MY EYES TO THE HILLS

An ordinary life in the hands of
an extraordinary God

Ethel Sibanda

Radiant
PUBLISHING FOR TRANSFORMATION

MY EYES TO THE HILLS

Radiant Publishing Company

PO Box BW 624,

Borrowdale, Harare

Zimbabwe

First Edition: 2020

ISBN: 978-1-77925-770-3

To my children and their spouses who have walked with me through thick and thin. And to my grand-children who are a great treasure and my life's delight.

ACKNOWLEDGEMENTS

It had never occurred to me that I could write a book. It was only through much persuasion from Barbara Nkala that I decided to share my sometimes difficult and deeply personal but hopefully God-glorifying life story. She and her sister Doris never stopped encouraging me along as I embarked on this project. My sincere gratitude to them.

I appreciate the family, friends and many people that God brought into my life and especially thank those who have written generous testimonials about me at the end of this book.

My family has not only been a source of information but have been my support and encouragement as they prayed for me throughout this work and without them, I would not have been able to complete the book. I am especially grateful to Seluleko and Siziwe who spent long hours, sometimes through the night, editing my writing.

Above all, I give praise and thanks to God my Father for enabling me to write this book.

CONTENTS

PREFACE

In many ways I have lived an ordinary life, a typical one for a woman of my generation, whose life crossed over from a rural colonial Zimbabwe to an independent one facing new and profound challenges.

As I look back however, I see how God has shaped the contours of the big decisions in my life and how He has been present in all its small moments. From a humble beginning in a rural subsistence farm to choices about life and work, the loss of my husband, living through the challenges of cancer and single parenthood, and to the joy of evangelism and grandchildren I have seen how God has been the author of my life and a constant presence. In the hands of this extraordinary God no life is truly ordinary, and I hope in sharing my story I will encourage you to look to Him even in the most difficult of times.

A great privilege of my life has been doing the work of evangelism. There is an urgent need for the church to share the gospel of Jesus with those who don't know Him. As Carl F. Henry once said, "The gospel is only good news if it gets there in time." In this book, I share experiences from my 17 years of working in evangelism ministry and some observations which I hope will be helpful to Christians and churches who want to respond in greater ways to the Great Commission.

To God be the glory!
Ethel Sibanda

FOREWORD

Jesus said, *"Anyone who loves his father or mother more than me is not worthy of me ... and anyone who does not take up his cross and follow me is not worthy of me"* (*Matthew 10:37, 38, NIV*). In the life of a committed Christian, love for the Lord is paramount. It affects one's family in every way, is based on the Word of God, depends on consistent and sincere prayer and results in effective witness and service. Ethel does a beautiful job of illustrating this as she tells her story in the following pages.

Strong Christian homes are the building block of any strong church and society. This was God's plan from the beginning of time. Christians must make their families a very high priority. Many Christians make ministry more important than family. They end up wondering why their children are negative and not strongly committed to the Lord. The story recorded in this book is a shining example of effective methods to develop a closely knit, loving family who remained concerned for and committed to each other up to the present. They still plan and enjoy family reunions.

Jesus stressed and personally personified the need to spend time in prayer. He knew that spending time alone with the Father was vital for his ministry. The Scriptures say that he went up into the mountain to pray. He said that one should enter his closet, shut the door and pray to the Father.

When reading the story of the Sibanda family, one cannot miss the importance of prayer in every situation. The children grew up practising this in every situation. It gave them peace and confidence in times of stress, including during the time of the loss of their father, relatives and friends. It also gave them guidance in times of uncertainty.

Giving the word of God high priority in life, especially in family life is absolutely essential in Christian living. The Lord told his people, *"Fix these words of mine in your hearts and minds; tie them as symbols on your hands and bind them on your foreheads. Teach them to your children, talking with them when you sit at home and when you walk along the road, when you lie down and when you get up. Write them on the doorframes of your houses and on your gates,"* (Deut. 11:18 – 20, NIV).

They made the word of God one of the most important things in their lives by insisting that any church which they attended taught what was true according the Scripture. Regular family devotions and memorizing scripture was naturally a part of their routine. Believing in the power of prayer brought peace and healing from an experience of severe cancer in the family.

Love for the Lord and one's family naturally results in wanting others to know and experience salvation. Ethel became an avid witness for the Master. Once while driving together to Botswana, we gave a total stranger a lift. She immediately began to witness to him about Jesus. Her enthusiasm for witnessing was apparent when she underwent Outreach Training and joined Evangelism Explosion, EE. When one is in ministry, teaching others and mentoring them becomes a great blessing, especially to see them grow and develop.

My relationship with Ethel started in 1960 when I taught her in

Form 1 at Matopo Secondary School. Thank you, Ethel for sharing the story of your life through this book. May it be a challenge
and encouragement to all who read it.

Jacob R Shenk

*Missionary in BICC Zimbabwe since 1958, and former Bishop (1994
– 1999)*

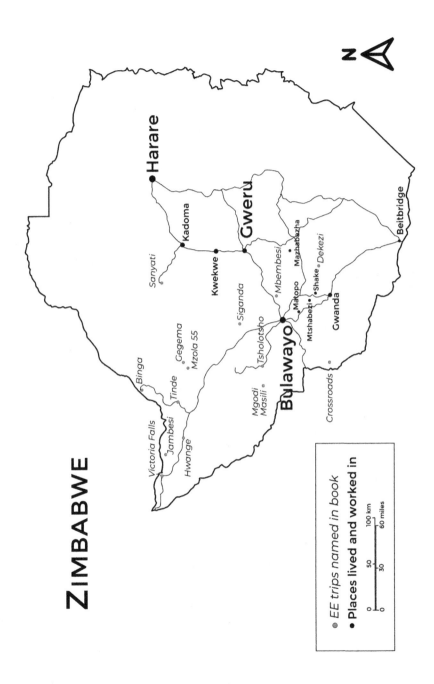

ZIMBABWE

Harare
Kadoma
Sanyati
Gweru
Kwekwe
Mbembesi
Mazhabazha
Siganda
Dekezi
Shake
Matopo
Gegema
Mzola 55
Tinde
Binga
Tsholotsho
Mtshabezi
Gwanda
Bulawayo
Mgodi
Masili
Victoria Falls
Jambesi
Hwange
Crossroads
Beitbridge

N

● EE trips named in book
● Places lived and worked in

0   50   100 km
0   30   60 miles

xi

1

EARLY LIFE

In 1931 Rev Harvey J Frey, a young American missionary with the Brethren in Christ Church opened a school in Mazhabazha, a small farming community two hours south-east of Bulawayo. He walked door-to-door, asking parents to allow their children to attend school, which was not easy because children were important in the working life of the family, performing such tasks as herding cattle, collecting firewood and working in the fields.

One of these parents, Mzondiwa Ndlovu, known as Makafula for his love of chewing tobacco, was then a father of 10 children, seven boys and three girls. Unsure of the value of the mission-ary's strange new idea and wary of losing the help of his children around the farm, he only reluctantly allowed his sons to attend. However, he refused to let his eldest daughter go to school. I am sure he was watching her grow, hoping she would get married and he would receive some cows for lobola (dowry), as was the norm for girls at the time. Rev Harvey J Frey or Mnali (Mis-sionary), as he was called in isiNdebele, did not give up. He re-turned to persuade Mzondiwa, who subjected him to a mini interview;

"Mnali what will you teach my daughter?"

Mnali replied, explaining what would happen at the school, and Mzondiwa listened carefully but still had one more question.

"Will she be good?"

He wanted to know if she would still grow to be a good wife. Mnali answered, "Yes, she will be good." After taking a puff on his pipe, Mzondiwa replied, "Ok, she can go to your school."

That daughter's name was Seke (also known as Neddie), and she was my mother. My name is Ethel Sibanda, born on 25 December 1944 to Majoni Sigwegwe and Seke Sibanda. I am the third oldest with two older brothers, three younger sisters and a younger brother who died aged two. At the time, polygamy was the norm, so I grew up with many brothers and sisters from my stepmothers.

We spent a happy childhood at our farm in Mazhabazha in the district of Filabusi, now known as Insiza. The farm was in the Gwatemba Purchased Areas, which included Gwatemba, Bungwe, Langeni and Mwele. My parents belonged to a Farmer's Union, which helped them operate commercially rather than for subsistence. Mazhabazha is named after a range of hills at the edge of our farm and which marked the boundary between Native Purchase Areas and commercial white farmland.

While writing this book, I was privileged to visit Messiah College in Pennsylvania, USA, home of the Brethren-In-Christ Church, which had sent missionaries such as Amos Ginder. Glen and Linda Pierce lovingly hosted me and arranged for me to see some of my old teachers and many of those who served in our Mission stations. Glen works at the Messiah College Library and

Archives of the Brethren-In-Christ Missions, and he kindly took me to his office where I learned much about the early work of the church and missionaries in Zimbabwe, some of which I will be sharing in my book.

First, I found out that the Purchased Areas that I mentioned above were called 'Gwatemba Native Purchased Areas'. These were small-scale farms that were bought by black farmers through a loan from the Government, which they repaid as they used the land. They were assisted by Field Administrators (*Abalimisi*) who educated them on animal husbandry. Twice a year, farmers like my father would bring their cattle to the market.

These Administrators also helped them with crop rotation so they would keep their fields productive every year and taught them how to use contour ridges to stop soil erosion. They would then send their crops to the Grain Marketing Board after harvest. The main cash crops were maize, finger millet (*uphoko*) and groundnuts. After the harvest, my father would hire a machine for separating the grain from the corn and another for shelling groundnuts to prepare them for sale.

We didn't use fertiliser on the farm but produced compost by putting maize stalks in the cattle kraal, which would then be trampled by the cows and mixed with their manure. There was no irrigation, so we depended on good rains which other than during a few years of drought were very reliable.

Like my mother, I also started my education at Mazhabazha School, a mile away from home. The school was founded by missionaries from the Brethren-In-Christ Church (BICC) who had already established institutions, called Missions, at Matopo, Mtshabezi and Wanezi. Each Mission had churches, schools and a clinic. Mazhabazha was under Wanezi Mission and was both a school and a church for us.

The gospel and education transformed people's lives, and their health improved by greater access to medical care. The school was like any other that the missionaries founded, but for me, it became the very source of my Christian journey. Before I proceed, I would like to share how the BICC came to be in Zimbabwe, for the benefit of those who might not know the roots.

Missionaries Come to Southern Rhodesia

I understand that at the annual conference of the Brethren-In-Christ Church in Pennsylvania in 1893, a lady stood up to suggest that the Church should take the gospel to Africa. The church declined to take this up, deciding that there remained much to do to spread the gospel in North America. The following year at the same General Conference, the same lady again stood up to implore the church to send missionaries to Africa. However, this time one of the delegates, Rev J.E. Stauffer stood and placed US$5 on the secretary's table stating that it was for foreign mission work. This challenge prompted more contributions, and the Conference commissioned a fundraising committee to start the work. In the archives, I counted it a privilege to not only to see but touch that special table, where the US$5 was placed.

Sufficient money had been raised by 1897 for a party of five, led by Jesse Engle, to make the month-long sailing to Cape Town, on the southern tip of Africa. By God's providence, the ship's captain knew a lot about Southern Africa. He advised them to go further inland northwards to Zimbabwe, then called Southern Rhodesia and a territory of Cecil John Rhodes' British South Africa Company.

He told them to take a train that would go straight from Cape Town to Bulawayo. That was God's plan because when they left America, they were just going to southern Africa but had no specific place in mind. In Cape Town, Cecil John Rhodes gave them a letter to the local Administrator informing him that they were Christian missionaries and instructing him to allocate some land to them.

When they arrived in Southern Rhodesia, they spent the first few nights at Solusi Mission about 50km east of Bulawayo, with Seventh-Day Adventist missionaries who had already settled there. The Administrator in Bulawayo allocated them 3000 acres in the Matopo Hills, 50km south of Bulawayo, where in 1898, they established Matopo Brethren-In-Christ Mission. However, the site was later moved to where Matopo Mission stands today. From there they established Mtshabezi and Wanezi Missions and then many schools in the province, including Mazhabazha in 1931.

Impact of Bible for Seke

My mother started going to school at about the age of 13 in 1931. At the time the missionaries taught students to read and write so they could read the Bible. What a strategy! I can still remember how my mother used to spell her words because of their alphabet (A –bhe – ce - de) for ABCD. After they had learnt to read and write, they received the New Testament that was available in Zulu, a dialect of isiNdebele. I remember my mother's Bible was black. She told me that they went through the four gospels three times a year in church, so learners had good grounding on the gospel of Jesus Christ. Even though she did not continue her education because she started school late, she had a deep understanding of the gospel.

When she married my father, they not only had a traditional ceremony but also celebrated a white (western) wedding ceremony in a church. This practice was relatively new and was an expression of faith for Christians in those early days of the gospel. No photos of the wedding remain, but I understand that she wore a white wedding dress, a white pair of tennis shoes and she held a white umbrella.

My uncle, Khutshwekhaya and other relatives who had come to Christ and had adopted this new way of life helped her in buying her wedding attire. My father had already been working in Bulawayo doing some general work, so he bought his own wedding suit.

When I was five, my mother taught me John 1: "In the beginning was the Word and the Word was with God and the Word was God". She would sit down with me and ask me to say the verse after her because I could not read at the time, but eventually, I could recite it from memory. I remember later as we were growing up whenever anyone did something wrong, she would say, "*IBhayibhili lithini? Ulibala njani?*" (What does the Bible say? How do you understand it?)

She would never miss a Sunday or mid-week service, Sunday school or Church conferences. She took seriously the vow that she had made at her baptism - that she would be faithful in attending all the church meetings. She would take us girls to church meetings all the time, but since my brothers were tending cattle, it was not always possible for them to come to church; however, we all went to Sunday school.

I have always traced God's work in my life back to my

mother's encounter with the missionaries. To me, it was no co-incidence that Harvey J Frey arrived just before my mother was too old to start school, where she heard the gospel, gave her life to Christ and brought us up to know and love Him. Jeremiah 1:5 says "Before I formed you in the womb I knew you, before you were born I set you apart..." (NIV). I believe this verse is true for my life, and I praise God for all He did to fulfil His plan through the many people who came before me.

Education

I started school in 1952 at the age of eight because one had to be able to touch their left ear with the right hand before they could enrol. That meant the taller children went to school earlier than the shorter children of the same age. The school buildings were used for both school and church, and the curriculum designed so that every day we started with Bible classes, which were called Biblical Instruction. Other subjects that we did in Sub Standard A and B were Vernacular (which was IsiNdebele), Reading, Writing, Arithmetic, Nature Study, Hygiene and Handwork which included craft for girls and some basic carpentry for boys.

I remember weaving floor mats and tablemats from wild grasses such as *imizi, isikusha, umnyankomo*. Nature Study included learning about the fly and its dangers to everyday life, plants and seasons of the year. From the archives of 1936 and 1937, I found out that Woodwork, Animal Husbandry, Forestry and Building were some other subjects taught.

In these elementary classes, Sub Standard A and B, teaching was in isiNdebele, and we wrote our work on slates. These were thin, flat, rectangular pieces of rock in a wooden frame on which we would write in chalk. After the teacher had marked it, we would erase the work to make space for the next lesson. The two disadvantages of the slate were that parents never saw our written work because at the end of the school day there is nothing on the slate except our last activity and that it was fragile, breaking into pieces whenever dropped, needing costly replacement. The walk home to tell my parents that I had broken my slate was always one made with great nervousness. Since money was not readily available, I would often go for days without anything to write on.

The following years were Standards One, Two and Three. We graduated to writing with a pencil in an exercise book and this felt like a big deal at the time. At that level, we had more responsibility around the school, especially on Fridays, because the classes had to be clean in preparation for Sunday services. There was one extra room just outside the school ground, which was used by the school manager and his wife for about two nights at a time when they visited the school. We had to clean the room and collect water and firewood for their use while they were at the school.

I am sure they brought stretchers with them because the room did not have a single item of furniture. I believe those were dedicated missionaries as it was not the most comfortable trip, visiting all the schools in the district. During that time, they would teach us some choruses in English. I remember one which to me sounded like "A little fountain upside down, everybody ought to be happy." Then later, when I understood English, I wondered how a fountain could be upside down?

2

GROWING TO KNOW THE LORD

I have always treasured Bible classes because they formed the basis of my understanding and love of the Bible. Although most of the teaching was in story form, it cultivated in me a love of God that I cherish to this day. Memorising scripture was a crucial part of Biblical Instruction classes. I still appreciate that because most of the verses that I know from memory today were learnt by heart in those days. Every Sunday morning, we went to church for Sunday school where we would sing choruses, learn a Bible story, learn and memorise a new verse and pray.

As we grew older, we would join the adults every Wednesday for a prayer meeting, which was like a Sunday service but shorter. When I visited the BICC archives at Messiah College in Pennsylvania a few years ago, I was thrilled to find records with names of all members of our local church and of those who attended baptism classes. I was delighted to see listed my mother, all my siblings and everyone that I grew up with. My prayer and hope is that all those names will also be found in the Book of the

Lamb.

Looking back, I am very grateful to all those who taught us at school and Sunday school. Teachers locally trained at newly established Brethren-In-Christ colleges later replaced the missionaries. They were expected to teach, give spiritual guidance and to live by example because they had come through the same system.

I continued attending church and all other church meetings, but at that time, I had no relationship with the Lord. I had started stealing things like sugar, eggs and other small items at home. One Sunday, our local preacher's sermon so convicted me that it seemed as though he was talking to me. So, at the end of the service I responded to an invitation to salvation at the age of 13. Typically, what then happened was that the pastor's wife would take the girls (while the pastor took the boys) and ask them to mention every sin they had committed. Then she would assure them that Jesus had died for their sins, and God had forgiven them.

My next step was to attend the baptism class, which was a two-year study of the BICC booklet, *Imibuzo LeMpendulo* (Questions and Answers), followed by baptism and church membership. I chose to be baptised, together with my younger sister Hilda who had also committed her life to Christ. To qualify for baptism, we had to pass a set of questions based on the study from the booklet. This was to make sure that we understood the gospel and the doctrine of the church. I appreciate that now because I can see the benefit in my life as it gave me a deeper grounding in the truth of God's Word.

Early School Days

My school went as far as Standard Three which was the end of Lower Primary School. After that, I went to Upper Primary School at Gwatemba School, the nearest school offering Standard 4. Doing so was an immense privilege since many children left at this stage as their parents either could not afford sending them to school, or because the school was too far. It could be as far as two and half hour walk one way. My father asked the Head of the school if I could live with him and his family in the teachers' accommodation, and he kindly agreed. His name was Mr James Nkala, and his wife was MaMoyo. There was a time when it was not convenient for me to stay with them, so I would leave home on my bike at 5.00 am arriving in time for school to start at 7.30 am. I was joined by my neighbour and classmate Sotsha Moyo. I completed Standards four and five there over two years.

At the time, I had a *mam'omcane* (aunt) who was attending boarding school at Mtshabezi. Her name was Senia Nsingo (nee Ndlovu). During the holidays she suggested that I ask my parents to send me to Mtshabezi Mission. The idea of going to boarding school excited me very much, but I was not sure if my parents could afford it. It prompted me, for the first time in my life, to pray deeply and in earnest. I did not know how to pray, but I would go out in the bush, kneel down and simply asked God if He could make it possible for me to go to Mtshabezi. I do not remember if I did that every day, but that was my first answered prayer, because I got a place to study Standard Six at Mtshabezi, and my parents were able to pay for me.

This prayer was a stepping-stone in my life because I got confidence that if I prayed, God would answer. In my journey of faith, you will note how many times God has answered my

My brother Enock, grandfather Makafula and sister Elsa in the early 70's

prayers.

Childhood on the Farm

Growing up on a farm that bordered the bush, we never lacked opportunities for fun and play. We enjoyed swimming in a small pool on the farm that my father later turned into a dam.

A range of hills at the bottom of the farm provided many opportunities for playing, picking wild fruit, collecting firewood and a shrub whose fibres were used for weaving mats.

Looking back, I see the protection of God because the area was teeming with venomous snakes, such as black mambas, some of which preyed on our chickens. But when we played, we did not encounter any. We played games like 'iguni', hide and seek and many others where all we needed was our enthusiasm and imagination. On rare occasions we would go and play with our neighbours' children; I say rare because there was always a lot of work to do at home and in the field.

The girls did all the household chores - cooking, washing dishes, collecting water and firewood - as part of our upbringing to prepare us for future roles as wives and mothers. There were times when we had to drive the cattle to the dip tank after my brothers left for boarding school at Wanezi Mission. I loved all those activities even though they were not always comfortable jobs, especially on rainy or chilly days. These were not without risk. Sometimes the cattle strayed into the crop fields which would land us in deep trouble. I remember getting a good hiding for that. We also learned to plough with oxen, either driving them or holding the plough.

There was a particular way of guiding the plough to avoid kinks in the furrows, known as amabhanga. Every child, boy or girl, had to learn that method as well as knowing how to space the seed evenly when sowing. One thing I could never learn to do was harness the oxen because I was afraid of approaching them. I did everything but that.

Christmas was our favourite time of the year, not only for its significance for Christians but also for the food and the treats we enjoyed then. It was the only time in the year we had bread and lots of it! Each family made a special order for Christmas, which would be collected from the local store on Christmas Eve. It would not feel like Christmas without that. I have fond memories of this delicious bread, topped with a red layer of Sun Jam and accompanied by Tanganda tea made with a lot of milk. This was my father's favourite tea and so was the only one we had at home.

Sometimes the Church would organise a communal party on Christmas day where everyone contributed beef, lamb or goat. After the Christmas meal, we would get our new clothes, much like children nowadays receive Christmas presents.

My birthday is on Christmas Day, but in those days, we did not celebrate birthdays the way we do today. I will always cherish memories of my mother taking us to church for a Christmas Day service where we would sing carols from the hymnal *Amagama Okuhlabelela*. That left a mark in my life because I do not ever remember not going to Church on Christmas Day. I treasure this legacy and have tried to pass it onto my own children. I pray that this tradition of honouring the Lord would continue through the coming generations.

My father was a subsistence farmer, so we worked hard to produce enough food to afford clothing and school fees. During the rainy season, from November to March, we grew maize, peanuts, round nuts (*indlubu*), rapoko (finger millet), pumpkins, watermelons, sweet potatoes, beans and a type of sugar cane known 'sweet reeds'. We spent most of the growing season weeding the crops. We all went to the fields early in the morning and worked happily together. It was not easy, but it was our way of life. We had a large herd of cattle, so we had a lot of milk at that time of year, some of which would be fermented into delicious curds (*amasi*).

We harvested green vegetables like pumpkin leaves, leaves from beans that would also be dried to provide relish in the summer months. We also enjoyed *ulude* (spider plant), a wild plant which grew after the first rains. It is still very much a staple of the Zimbabwean diet. In addition to produce from the ground, the seasons also brought many wild fruits. In the rainy season, we relished wild fruits like *umviyo, umlugulu, isigangatsha* and *amaganu*, fruit from the marula tree from which we brewed a very sweet drink. In the dry season, we had *umqokolo, umhlali, umkhemeswane* and many others. I have fond memories of an idyllic childhood.

3

BOARDING SCHOOL

Attending a mission boarding school was considered an incredible privilege. They were better resourced and offered a better education than local day schools. As a result, they attracted students from across the country, which created a more stimulating environment. Also, there was more time to devote to our studies without a long walk to school and farm work afterwards.

So, it was with great excitement that in 1959 it was time to pack for boarding school. I asked my *mam' omcane* Senia for a list of things that I would need, especially those that were not on my acceptance form. My budget was very tight due to the higher expense of boarding school and travel, so I only had the bare minimum required for my new school life. My mother used to make clay pots which she sold to help pay for fees and clothing.

The day came, and I left with as much food as I could carry for what was the longest journey I had ever taken and the longest time I had ever spent away from my family. I remember the mixed feelings of both anxiety and excitement going through my mind when I left for Mtshabezi. Life would never be the same again.

The first leg was a three-hour trip to Bulawayo in the back of a lorry used to ferry grain to market. It was owned by the Mkhwananzi family, who kindly allowed farmers in the community to use it. I had never been to a city, and the whole journey was a fantastic adventure. I then boarded a bus, for the first time in my life, to Mtshabezi. Fortunately, I was travelling with my aunt, and so I did not have to be anxious about anything but was able to enjoy the experience.

I clearly remember approaching the city at night and seeing the glow of the streetlights, which seemed as numerous as the stars in the sky. They looked as if they were on the ground and I wondered if there was any room for people to walk! Oh, I held my breath and never said a word until we were close enough, then I realised that the lights were in straight lines and there were roads in between. "Now this is the city, I have arrived at last," I thought with a sigh of relief. But I had yet to see and learn much more. These lights could not be blown out like candles or put out like fire at home, but they were switched on and off by pressing some knob with a click! Water came from a tap. I do not use a cup to scoop it from a big container. Wow!

In the morning, we continued to Mtshabezi by bus, which was a day's journey and an incredible adventure for me. It all seemed too good to be true. I still could not believe I was at boarding school until registration when we paid our fees and received uniforms and books. I was at the famous Mtshabezi Mission! God had answered my prayer and allowed me to go there. I was very grateful.

I relied on my loving aunt to guide me through the early days of my new school life. She also protected me from older students who took pleasure in teasing newcomers. This was a common practice that was sometimes quite horrible for the younger student. Soon however, I found my way around and enjoyed my classes and daily routine.

When all the excitement had died down, I realised that I would not be seeing my parents for another three and a half months and this was difficult for me. It was then that I truly missed home and felt quite lonely. Part of it was the diet - food cooked for hundreds of people in massive pots tasted different from what I was used to at home. I disliked bathing in cold water in the morning, but I had to adjust quickly because that was boarding school life. Anyway, life went on, and I soon made new friends who made the experience very enjoyable.

Life at School

There were two classes in Standard Six, which was the last of the primary school years. I was in Standard 6a, taught by our gentle teacher Mr Mkubo Dube (Bekithemba Dube's father). We split our time between academic study, which I much enjoyed, and manual work on the school farm, such as picking vegetables and guavas from the orchard and grinding nuts to make peanut butter. All these were to supply the school kitchen. The sport we played the most was netball which I loved because I used to play that at Gwatemba School. In athletics, I was an average middle-distance runner - my strength was in the sprint races, which I sometimes won.

At the end of the year, I passed and qualified to go to Matopo Secondary School, which at the time was the only BICC high school. I was now used to boarding school, so it was just a case of becoming familiar with the new surroundings and the school routine. Matopo had better school and boarding facilities than Mtshabezi. I studied six academic subjects, including Latin and two practical subjects, cookery and sewing. Even though Latin was called a dead language, I found it very beneficial in that the roots of most English words came from Latin. Later in life, I found that I could understand specific English terms that would otherwise have been tricky to understand.

In sewing class, we each made ourselves a dress, which counted towards our grade at the end of the year. Bishop Shenk, who decades later was in my church homegroup, taught me Science, and I was sorry to not do well in his subject because he was a good teacher. His dear wife, Nancy Shenk, taught us music. Staff notation was not easy for us because at the time we used to read Tonic Solfa notes. She was left-handed, and it was fascinating to see her writing on the chalkboard because, in our culture, it was taboo to use the left hand for writing, and especially for eating.

On the sports field, we took part in athletics and netball. I was part of the school team that travelled to compete with urban schools at White City Stadium, the largest athletics arena in Bulawayo. It was an exciting experience for me, and I'm sure for all my colleagues. I cannot recall whether there were some of us in the team who came first, but I remember coming third in my sprint event. I am sure that was the best I ever did.

Meeting Ferdinand

My memories of Matopo Secondary School are precious to me not just because of the happy years I spent there but also because that is where I met the love of my life, Ferdinand Kesari Sibanda, who later became my husband. It might sound strange now, but we only saw each other during term time because when schools closed, he would return to his home in Gwanda while I went back to Filabusi, 100 km away. During the holidays, we wrote letters to each other. A letter would take a week to arrive at its destination.

At school, we communicated by letters passed through our classmates. Boys and girls were not allowed to interact other than with one's classmates, and since he was two years ahead of me, we were not able to talk during term time. The only occasion boys and girls were able to speak was when the guy asked for permission from the school, allowing the two of you to meet near the Principal's residence for a limited time at weekends. We never took this opportunity because we found it culturally inappropriate to be public about our relationship. Of course, courtship looks very different now, but this was all we knew and were very happy with it.

School life at Matopo helped to grow my spiritual life and deepen my faith. Scripture was one of our core subjects, and it deepened my understanding of God's Word and of what the Lord Jesus had done for me. I was part of a quartet that was coached by Mrs Musser, the Principal's wife at the time. We sang in church regularly and even though we did not read music, we were able to learn our parts as she played the piano. The songs that I sang in the quartet and during Sunday worship have comforted, ministered, and revealed God's love to me over the years. I am ever so grateful to those who taught us the songs and to the Lord who filled them with meaning. It was at Matopo, where I made lifelong friendships.

God Directs my Early Career

After two years, I completed my RJC (Rhodesia Junior Certificate), which I found challenging, but by God's grace passed well. Continuing to Form Three and Form Four was impossible because some of my siblings had also started high school, and my parents could not afford for us all to go to boarding school. Instead, I decided to do a vocational course so I could work and help my parents. My best friend, Bessie Mkwananzi, who was a year ahead of me, had chosen nurse training at Mpilo Hospital in Bulawayo.

She desperately wanted me to join her there, and without putting much thought into whether or not it was right for me, I agreed. This was against my mother's advice, who felt that I would not be suited to the profession. Bessie helped me with the application, and in no time, I underwent medical examinations, which was the next step in the process. The results would take some time to come, so I decided to look for employment while I was waiting.

I went to the BICC education offices in Bulawayo to apply for a temporary teaching position. On the same day Rev George Bundy, the Schools Manager of Wanezi District was in the office and had a vacancy at Mbawulo School. He offered me the position and kindly gave me a lift to the District office, where I signed my contract. I was very thankful that the Lord had prepared something for me in such a short time. I signed on a Saturday, and I was to report for work on Monday, but I still had to go home to let my parents know and to collect my belongings.

I left Wanezi in the late afternoon on foot, running most of the way because the sun was low, it would soon be dark, and I was afraid of snakes. After two and a half hours, I reached Gwatemba Store, which was less than halfway home. By God's provision, Mkhwananzi's truck was ferrying farmers from a field day in Godlwayo, in southern Filabusi. He had stopped for refreshments and was about to leave when I arrived at sunset.

Mkhwananzi offered me a lift to Gwatemba School, which was his final destination. One of the farmers in the truck was my uncle, so I was glad to have someone to walk with for the next two and a half hours of my journey. When we arrived at his home, at about 9 pm, he compelled me to spend the night there, rather than walk the remaining 15min of my journey home. I lay in bed restless, counting all I had to do at home before leaving for Mbawulo the following morning. Even though he did it for my safety, I was very disappointed with him. After some time, I fell asleep because I was exhausted.

I was up before anyone else the following morning but waited to thank my uncle's family before walking home. My parents were surprised to see me that early as they thought I was in Bulawayo. They were more surprised when I told them about the job and that I had to leave within the next two hours. Oh, how I wish the days of mobile phones had come!

All the same, my Lord was there to see me through as my parents asked my brother Lameck (later known as *Seka* Sipho) to take me on a bicycle to catch the bus nearly 20 km away. We must have looked a sight with me carrying my suitcase and bedding on the back of a bike! I arrived at my destination in the evening, having caught two buses and relied on the driver to drop me off at Mbawulo as I had never been there before. Thankfully, the school was only a short walk from the bus stop. I met the headmaster, whose family kindly hosted me for a few weeks while the school committee found me a host family to live with. This arrangement was typical in most rural schools.

My First Job

This was my first job, the first time I taught and my first time living away from home as an adult, so it took some time for me to settle into life at Mbawulo. After settling down, I enjoyed it and loved the children. Recently, I met one of my pupils from that school who had later graduated as a teacher. He told me that some of his grandchildren had graduated from university, which made me proud as his former teacher.

I was posted to Mkwabeni Primary School, a neighbouring school, at the end of my first year. It was a bigger school with more staff who were very kind and helpful to me. Two of those were my aunt, who had paved the way for me to attend Mtshabezi, and her husband. I lived with them in their married teachers' accommodation for the duration of my time at Mkwabeni. Although I had appreciated my host family at my previous school, it was a delight to live with family.

Meanwhile, the medical examination results for my nursing application were out. I was offered a place at Mpilo Hospital in 1962. I was due to start in August of the same year, so I had very little time to confirm my acceptance. For some reason that I cannot explain, I just did not respond even though in my mind, I was still counting on that as my career.

One day the District schools' manager, Joe Ginder, arrived at the school on one of his regular visits. He asked what my plans were, and I told him that I was waiting to start my nurse training. He suggested that I consider attending teacher training at Mtshabezi, then the only teacher training college for BICC schools.

I had never considered a career in teaching. He promised that if I wished to attend Mtshabezi, I would not have to apply, but he would put my name on the list for the following year's intake. I must have given him an affirmative answer in our brief but consequential conversation, but I do not remember giving him the go-ahead response. Although I felt that I still wanted to accept Mpilo's offer, I started to seriously consider whether or not nursing was the right choice for me and began to pray about it. I found a spot in the nearby bush where on my knees, I asked God to guide me to the right decision.

However, as the days went on, I felt less and less sure about which of these two careers was right for me. One day, I received two letters in the mail, one from Mpilo Hospital notifying me that they had withdrawn my offer because I had not responded, the other from Mtshabezi Mission offering me a place at their next intake. To me, this was not just coincidence, it was God answering my prayer, so I had peace of mind about attending teacher training. In those days, mail took weeks to arrive so to have the two letters delivered at the same time was to me, a clear answer from God.

I continued teaching at Mkwabeni until the end of the year. BICC schools emphasise Christian teaching, so we attended Sunday services and midweek meetings, both of which helped to steadily grow my faith.

A Sad Event

Meanwhile, Ferdinand and I were still in love and continuing our relationship by writing letters to each other. That year, he lost his dearly-loved younger brother Ginder, who was studying Form Three at Matopo Secondary School. He fell ill at school and was taken to Mpilo Hospital where he died after a few days. I shared his grief and brokenness because Ginder and I had been in the same class for our first two years at Matopo.

It was difficult as I could not share my distress with my aunt and her husband, who I was living with at the time because culturally, I could not disclose my relationship with Ferdinand. I remember feeling lost and lonely, unable to be with Ferdinand at such a distressing time for him and his family.

The year and my stay at Mkwabeni soon came to an end. I bade the staff and my aunt's family farewell as I was leaving for teacher training at Mtshabezi. I had not only enjoyed my time there but also bought myself a new bicycle, which was my first investment. I had been able to save some money to pay for part of my training, which was a big help for my parents.

4

TEACHER TRAINING

After the excitement of Christmas, 1964, it was time to return to Mtshabezi Mission, this time for two more years to attend teacher training. Exciting! Incidentally this time I went with my younger sister, Hilda, who was starting her teacher training at the same time. Training was provided for Upper and Lower Primary teachers. Having completed my RJC; I qualified to teach in Upper Primary school. After living away from home for three years, I was glad to have my sister at school with me.

Mtshabezi was familiar to me from my time as a primary school student, but my experience of it was very different now as a mature student. The Principal at the time was Glen Fry, whose wife Mrs Fry had been born at Mtshabezi. Much had improved since my time there - more facilities and better food, for instance. Looking back, I appreciate my time at Mtshabezi because I see it as an essential part of God's plan for my life. I came to realise that it was more than just a career, but preparation for the education of children. I also saw it as a way of living life as an example of a Christ-follower. As soon as I started my supervised teaching practice, I felt that this was the right career for me. I relished it, loved the children, and I believed that I was just where God wanted me to be. My mind went back to my conversation with Joe Ginder at Mkwabeni, and I praised God for using him to lead me to the right career.

I began to have a greater sense of God's hand, leading and guiding me in my everyday life. I shared much of my school life with my close friend Hilda Ncube, who has since gone to be with the Lord. We had been classmates at Matopo, but now she was a class ahead of me because of the year I spent working. She was then the head girl, very patient with a lovely personality. There were only a few girls in my class, and we were all friends, it felt like being part of a family. I sang in a quartet with Vani Ndlovu, Gladys Moyo, and Ranna Khanye and we were coached by Miss Mann, a missionary at the school. Our voices blended very well together, and I remember a time we did a recording for Rhodesia Broadcasting Corporation.

Our time was split between academic study and teaching practice, which always took place at the primary school located between the high school and staff housing. For my final exam, I taught a geography lesson observed by the examiner, an Inspector from the Ministry of Education. Even though we were a Mission school, a government official had to conduct the final exam. The lesson went exceedingly well - I felt the Lord was with me and this, together with the Inspector's positive comments afterwards, strengthened my sense of calling as a teacher.

Our activities outside the classroom were mainly chores and sport. In my final year, on Saturday mornings, I was assigned to iron the female teachers' laundry, which I preferred to manual work on the school farm. Saturday was also when we prepared our school uniforms for the following week.

For girls, this included a white head wrap, *iqhiye,* which we stiffened by starching then tied in a specific way which allowed it to keep its form for the week. For some girls the head-wrap was too tricky to fold and secure on their own, so they asked others to do it for them. The drawback was that it took the shape of the head of the person who had tied it. I was one of those who relied on others to knot it for me, but later I managed to do it on my own. In the student dormitories, we used flat cast iron irons. These were heated on stoves and were more challenging to use, unlike those we used to iron the teachers' clothes.

During my final two terms, I was the school head girl. One of my more demanding roles was making sure that the girls were present and in an orderly queue before mealtimes and church meetings. Others were more routine, such as making announcements. All of this developed and gave me confidence as a leader, something which years later, I saw as God shaping me for ministry.

A Taste of Outreach Evangelism

During this time, we received a visit from a South African evangelist, Shadreck Mohanoe Maloka who brought a team to conduct a revival - a week of nightly meetings where he preached the gospel. He had a compelling testimony of having been abandoned as a toddler and grown up into gang culture before being saved. Because we were a mission school, many students were religious, but through his preaching and testimony, many were brought into relationship with Christ. Sometimes it takes a revival to bring such moments.

Me (centre) with Hilda and Ami at Mtshabezi High School (1964)

I remember after that how easy it was to get everyone to queue and on time. It was incredible. The evangelism team also taught us new Zulu choruses that we still sing to this day such as *'Akungenwa lemithwalo'* (No baggage when heaven bound); and *'Mzalwane usithathaphi isibind' esingaka'* (Beloved,what courage is that?) and many others. A lady who was part of the team shared a dream that she had where she saw me holding different kinds of fruit, saying that she believed it meant that I would bear fruit in serving the Lord. This event made a big impression on my life. I saw the transformation that the gospel could bring to people's lives, and it gave me a passion for evangelism that would stay with me for life.

The summer of 1964 brought mine and Hilda's graduation as trained teachers. It was a memorable occasion for us even though our parents were not able to attend. In those days, very few parents could make it to graduation. However, we were delighted that my uncle, my mother's brother, and his wife, Mr and Mrs Jack Diza (JD) Ndlovu, were able to attend. He was a teacher at Matopo Secondary School, and they came to Mtshabezi as if to represent our parents, who could not be there. It was precious, and we have always cherished that.

We returned home after graduation to Christmas festivities that were even greater and more joyous than usual. Even extended family joined in celebration and thanksgiving to God for His grace towards us. My mother's sister provided a goat for the occasion.

Life as a Teacher

Before the holidays we had been assigned to the schools where our teaching careers would begin. I was appointed to Mtshabezi Primary School, a place I was very familiar with having completed my teaching practice there. Hilda was posted to Mazhabazha Primary, our home school where my mother had started her education all those years ago. This meant that she would live with my parents, who were glad at the news as she had grown up with a persistent cough, which years later was diagnosed as an allergy.

It was strange returning to Mtshabezi as a teacher having been a student only a month before. It was an honour, especially to be appointed to a Mission school, and I had a deep sense of responsibility as a role model and of the influence that this position gave me. I lived with three other female teachers in the staff quarters who I later formed strong friendships with. We lived as a family - sharing the cooking, meals and our recreational time which was a blessing to me.

The primary school was a fair distance away so we all purchased bicycles through the mission account, to which we made monthly repayments. It was exciting to be earning a salary again. We looked forward to the end of the month, where we would make a shopping trip to Bulawayo. I tried to save money to take home to my parents at the end of the term.

I was assigned to teach a Standard Four class which I enjoyed very much. This was a morning class, which finished at 1.00 pm. Those who are teachers will know the work involved after school - marking and planning for the following day. There were two boys in that class who were so smart that I had high hopes of seeing them go through University. Sadly, when I met them both later in life, they had not been able to continue their education for one reason or another.

In addition to my regular class on two days a week, I

taught an afternoon Std. 4 class from 2 to 4 pm. This was known as hot-sitting - children with less academic ability attended in the afternoon because there was not enough room to accommodate every child in the morning classes. They did fewer subjects and spent less time at school, but I loved this class because it gave an opportunity to children that would otherwise have dropped out of school.

One afternoon while standing in front of the class I experienced a blackout. My vision slowly grew dimmer, and the children appeared as if they were drifting further away. I managed to sit down and dismissed the class. The next thing I remember was opening my eyes in the headmaster's office, surrounded by most of the staff. My headmaster was Baba Samuel Mlotshwa, a compassionate and accommodating man. My uncle, Bishop Stephen Ndlovu and his dear wife Ottilia were also staff, and they took me to the Mission hospital, but by then, I was feeling better. The doctor examined me, and nothing showed up. As I look back, I believe that this is one of those times when the Lord intervened for the sake of His plans and purposes for my life.

5

THE WEDDING

In the meantime, my relationship with Ferdinand continued to deepen as we corresponded by mail. Receiving his letters was always a joy, and I loved hearing about his thoughts and life at school and later on at work. Having completed his 'O' Levels at Matopo, he was accepted for 'A' Level study at Goromonzi High School. This was an outstanding achievement because that was the only government school in Rhodesia that black students could attend to prepare for University, so the entry standards were very high.

However, he had only been there for two weeks before he made the difficult decision to give up this opportunity and find work. His mother needed help with school fees for his siblings, who wouldn't have been able to continue their education because of a change in his parents' circumstances. He found a job as a temporary teacher in Ratanyana, an hour beyond Matopos in the mopane woodlands of Matabeleland South. While teaching there, he secured a position at Rhodesia Broadcasting Corporation (RBC) at their Bulawayo Studios on the old Jameson Road, where the Adventist Church currently is.

We had been courting for six years by then and around that time decided to get married. Our letters were increasingly about plans for our wedding and life afterwards. Some of his siblings had since left school, so he felt he was in a better position financially for marriage. So, in 1965 the traditional wedding preparations, including the payment of amalobolo (lobola), took place with plans that the wedding would take place in April 1966.

Meanwhile, Hilda had found the love of her life, Gideon Moyo, a physiotherapist who worked at Jairos Jiri Rehabilitation Centre in Bulawayo. They wanted to get married as soon as possible, and so my parents asked Ferdinand to rearrange our wedding for August later that year. Before I knew it, I was busy looking for a wedding dress and buying material and having dresses made for my six bridesmaids. There was a small boutique in the city-centre of Bulawayo called Joyettes that had very fashionable wedding dresses. It was there that I chose a beautiful lace wedding gown. Now that I was working, I was able to fully pay for it in two months, something I was proud of.

It was customary for the bride-to-be to visit the groom's home before the wedding to officially meet her in-laws. Therefore, sometime in July, a month before the wedding, my friend Iris Ncube, who I taught and lived with, accompanied me to Ferdinand's home in Shake (pronounced Sha-ké) for the weekend. I was excited, but having never met Ferdinand's parents, Kesari and Eve Sibanda, I was anxious. My fears turned out to be unwarranted as they were both lovely people. When we arrived, we received a warm and loving welcome, or as we say in isiNdebele, 'ngezandla zombili' (with both hands). I cannot put in words my feelings at the time - how precious those moments were. This moment was a long time coming, after six years of a long-distance relationship, our dream was coming true. My heart was full of praise to God. I had a praying mother, and my future mother-in-law was also a devout woman of prayer. I am grateful to God for the gift of these two precious mothers in my life, whose prayers brought Ferdinand and I together and sustained our marriage.

Ferdinand drove Iris and I back to Mtshabezi, but on the way, we visited Lumene to meet his maternal grandparents. It was proper for them to meet the woman who was going to be the wife of their grandson, the first one to get married. They too were delighted to meet me as I was them. I was sad to part with Ferdinand as he returned to Bulawayo but excited about our future together.

Wedding Day

The days rolled by, and the wedding day finally arrived. Rev Sandi Vundla married us at Mpopoma BIC Church on Thursday 31 August 1966. It was terrific to march into a church as a bride because I had always prayed to be married in a Christian ceremony, saying our vows before God. Another couple was getting married in the same ceremony, and we marched into church one after the other. This wasn't unusual as Rev Vundla was the only BIC marriage officer in the city churches and August was a popular time for weddings. He preached one sermon and then performed our vows separately. After the ceremony, we went to a famous studio in the city centre, African Photos, to take our wedding pictures. Afterwards, we went back to Mpopoma for lunch at my husband's uncle's house - Jonathan Nyoni, better known as *uSeka* Carter. His wife was a great cook, and so the food was delicious.

Our wedding day (1966)

Traditionally the wedding reception took place in two parts - at the bride's home without the in-laws and then at the groom's homestead with everyone. After lunch, we made the two-hour journey to Mazhabazha with the wedding party for the following day's celebration. The car that we were travelling in broke down halfway at Mbalabala and experienced a long delay as we waited for parts from Bulawayo.

We arrived home in the early hours of the morning, so we didn't get much sleep. Our local pastor, Thomas Moyo and his wife, MaMpofu, who was my mother's best friend, hosted us. I still remember how the family did their best to provide everything we needed most - warm baths and breakfast. This was no small sacrifice on their part because we were a large group.

Around noon we made our traditional processional entry to my home, the beloved farm where I was born and raised and had often dreamt about a day such as this. I was arriving home as a bride, and my parents would see me in this beautiful white dress which even my mother had not seen. What a day! We were blessed to have a bright and sunny day, almost too hot under the afternoon sun. It was one of the first few weddings in my home area, where the bridal party performed choreographed steps to entertain the guests. Our dancing was well received by the guests, in particular the *'Azingene!'* done to symbolise the welcoming of the amalobolo cattle as they arrive from the groom's family.

We were all having such a wonderful time. I remember the best man, my husband's best friend Daniel Ndlela, telling the rest of the bridal team to do their best because that day would never come back. How true this was. We were very grateful to him for making our day so unique and memorable. While the guests enjoyed the wedding feast, the bridal team savoured a meal specially prepared by oMaNkala, Mrs Alice Ndlovu and Mrs Otilia Ndlovu, my uncles' wives. This was a highlight which I remember with fondness. There was plenty of food, as my father had provided a cow for the feast, which was important to him. It is believed that slaughtering a cow or any livestock for such an event is a blessing, a happy send-off.

After the meal, my cousin Mikha Khutshwekhaya Ndlovu gave a speech on behalf of the family, speaking words that I have always kept in my heart. He said that since I would be living with a family that we did not know, my role would be to nurture the relationship between the two families, uniting them in friendship instead of enmity. The day ended with us thoroughly exhausted but having had a wonderful time. Opening my eyes, the following morning, I remember thinking to myself, "Ah, this is a different day! I am actually leaving my mother. Suddenly mixed feelings of excitement and fear filled my heart. Change is not always easy; the thought of facing the unknown and starting life in a new environment with new people overwhelmed me. I had no time to dwell on this; however, it would soon be time to leave for the next leg of the wedding celebrations at Ferdinand's home. A new chapter had begun.

Before we left, I took part in a traditional meeting, *ukulaya,* where my aunties and other female relatives counselled me on what to expect and what was expected of me in marriage. I received much advice that helped me as a young daughter in-law and in particular from my aunt. She said that I must not forget that as an in-law I would always be a 'visitor', therefore before I said a word, I should ask myself if that word was appropriate for a 'visitor' to say. I cherish that guidance as it stopped me from saying unbefitting words many times when I was unsure whether to speak or be quiet.

There was one last thing to be done before we left - following custom I walked through the cattle kraal (pen) with my brother Edgar holding my hand. The dam of my emotion at departing from home burst open, and I cried the whole way. This rite of parting made everything seem so final. I was leaving not just the only home I had ever known but my family, neighbours, relatives and church community for good. I didn't understand it at the time, but this was something I needed to do as part of the process of leaving home and joining a new family.

The Celebration Moves to Shake

After a whirlwind 24 hours in Mazhabazha, we left for Shake, accompanied by a sizeable crowd of my relatives (*umthimba*), arriving at noon. We went to the local primary school, Shake School, to get dressed for the celebration. Culturally, it was a significant wedding because Ferdinand was the firstborn, as was his father, so it had drawn relatives from far and wide and many people from the community.

USeka Ferdinand (my father-in-law) had been the head-teacher at the school for several years, and Naka Ferdinand (my mother-in-law) was still teaching there, so they were well-known. Once we were ready, we entered the homestead to much ululation, dancing and celebration. There were joyous cheers of '*Woza laye!*' meaning come, bring her home. For both of us, this was one of the happiest moments of our wedding.

It was not typical or expected for the bride to be smiling and looking around. One was expected to be sober and respectful. Perhaps sober may not be the right word, but to be the bride that people expected to see. It would have been embarrassing for the bride to look all over and smile. That was the expectation, and for me, I was too scared even to look up. Nowadays, it is different as brides smile and talk. It looks good and is fun. Many things change with time.

After the grand entry, we sat down to eat. My in-laws had gone out of their way to prepare a wonderful feast. My husband, being a broadcaster, had been working with many music artists, so he had hired an '*imbube*' group to entertain our guests. Those who are my age might remember the group called 'Crown Figure'. They were very popular at the time, and having only heard them on the radio, our guests were delighted to see them perform live.

My husband's uncle, Jacob Mondi Nyoni, spoke on behalf of the family. He told my husband to work hard because it would not be acceptable for me to maintain the size of dress that I was wearing after marriage. "Your wife must look nourished," he said. The understanding then was that my not gaining weight would be a sign that he was not looking after me well. Those were the days! The celebration continued into the night with the music group singing until the early hours of the morning.

The following morning there was the traditional hand-over ceremony, where my family officially presented me to my new family, and Ferdinand's *ukulaywa* (marriage advice) took place. After that my people returned to Mazhabazha, which for me was also a sad parting as I said goodbye to them all. Only my younger sister Elsa remained as part of a custom to help me during the first days at my new home. We were all tired and enjoyed the quiet and rest having had what seemed like one long celebration over the previous four days.

We spent a few days in Shake before leaving for Bulawayo for three days for a brief honeymoon before returning. We lived with his parents, which was not difficult as they were easy going. For example, culturally, it was considered inappropriate for me to dine in the same room as my mother or father-in-law for a period after joining the family. As a kind gesture, my in-laws paid me a small fee to undo the law, something I much appreciated.

A New Life in the City

When the school holidays were over, I returned to Mtshabezi to finish off the year and say my farewells before joining my husband in Bulawayo. During the Christmas holidays, we went home to help with work in the fields as was common in those days. According to our custom, the eldest son had to leave his parents' home and build his own.

We had just started planning that when a family nearby announced that they were moving and selling their home. Even though we were not ready to build, we bought their house and fields. It took us many years to build our house because we spent most of our time in the Bulawayo where we also had bought a house, in Mpopoma. We were starting afresh because the previous owners had demolished all their buildings. In those days it was customary to not erect a home in the same spot where a house had stood, so we built our four-roomed house on a rock at the edge of the property.

6

FAMILY

On the afternoon of 26 June 1967, we were blessed with our first-born son Sijabuliso (Sja or CJ) at Mpilo Hospital. His birth brought great joy to both families as he was the first grandchild on both sides of the family. I had a long labour and that with the challenges of nursing in the early days left me exhausted. Thankfully both our mothers were there to support and help me. Even after seven children, I remember it like it was yesterday since every birth was unique.

I had not been able to return to teaching because there were only a few schools in the city, all run by the City Council, and there were no BIC mission schools. Not only that, but a municipal policy to discourage black families settling in the city meant that every female teacher was a temporary teacher. Therefore, if you went on maternity leave, you had to re-apply as a new employee, and older women past childbearing age and men occupied all the teaching places. I now faced a dilemma and had to choose between living unemployed in town with my husband or at a mission school where I could teach. Around that time in 1968, my husband was transferred to Harare (Salisbury, at the time) for about a year. We moved there and lived with Christopher Sibanda's family, who was married to my husband's cousin Addis Mtshazo. Christopher, who was a well-known broadcaster and also employed at ZBC, had been transferred to Bulawayo.

Learning to Depend on God

We soon rented a house in Mufakose, a new township on the eastern outskirts of Harare. I did not speak Shona at the time, so I had a difficult time finding my way around, attending the baby clinic and making friends. However, I settled well as time went on. I did not stay in Harare for long, however, as I became unwell. I had no pain, but I felt weak, sometimes unable even to hold my baby. One Saturday afternoon, my husband had planned to go and watch a soccer match but was unable to because I could not pick up CJ, who was less than a year old. My family decided that I should go back to Shake where I would have help and support during the week. It was sad to be apart from my husband so early in my marriage, but we felt that we were making the right decision.

I stayed with my mother-in-law, who was gracious and generous at a time when she faced challenges of her own. My strange symptoms continued, and one day we hired a car to Gwanda Hospital, about an hour away, but the doctors could not find anything wrong with me. My pulse and blood pressure were fine. That was one of the times I remember calling on the Lord in prayer. I had always maintained a prayer life, but I had never faced such a difficult challenge, and my petition became more personal and desperate. I could not work in the fields, where help was needed most, but stayed behind to prepare meals instead. It might have seemed unfair to the others, and I felt inadequate as a daughter-in-law, that I was not fulfilling my traditional role.

I had always expected to get help from the hospital, but when the doctors could not find the problem life felt uncertain, and I did not know where to turn. A local traditional healer *(inyanga)* suggested that he could help with my mysterious illness. I felt helpless and was still immature in my faith, so I consented to his idea and took his potion. He also claimed to know who was responsible for my illness. He said the weirdest things that my husband and I knew were not true. I believe this was God showing us not to trust in man but in Him.

This incident led me to search the Bible and I realised it was a sin to use *inyanga*. I made up my mind that from that day on, I would never consult these people again. Anyway, over the next few months and without any medication, I gradually got better. O how God loves us! He could have healed me before I visited *inyanga*, but He wanted me to know that my life was truly in His hands.

In that same year, 1968, I secured a teaching post at our neighbouring school, Zhugwe, which was a 90-min cycle away. During the week, CJ was looked after by his grandmother while I lived at the school, cycling home on weekends. On Sundays, I attended church at Shake BICC, which met at the school. I was asked to teach adult Sunday school and enjoyed the class, partly as it was an opportunity to know my new church family better. I had met most of them after the wedding, but because we lived in the city, I had not met them as often. Their participation was enthusiastic and confirmed to me that God was using my gift of teaching. Discussions were very lively, and the teaching staff participated, which kept the class engaging well.

A Change of Direction

Life was demanding with my husband now returned to Bulawayo from Harare, my son in Shake and me in Zhugwe. We decided that I would do a course that would help me to find employment in the city. In 1970 I completed a one-year course in clothing, pattern-making and grading. After the training, I obtained a job at Femina Garments doing exactly that, and this gave me valuable experience in working in the clothing industry. I found it to be a very different environment from teaching. I had always been employed in Christian schools, and the change to an urban and secular workplace was a challenging adjustment for me to make. The language, conversations and behaviour of my workmates and how employers treated the workers made me feel out of place as a Christian. I was delighted to be with my husband again, living together as a family, and this helped me to quickly adjust to my new work situation.

We attended our nearest BIC Church, Mpopoma. I soon liked it and made it my home church. It was not long before I joined all the wonderful and faithful women who had been teaching children's Sunday school for many years. I remember Mrs Abbie Dube, late Mrs Grace Mzizi, Mrs Zama Ncube, the late Mrs Rita Mabhena, late Mrs Maphosa, Mrs Mchindu and Mrs O Moyo. They were a united group from whom I learnt a lot as a young mother.

A Lesson in Contentment

In my new neighbourhood, Mpopoma, there was a young guy who came from Shake, and we became friendly with him. He

Ferdinand in the late 1970's

survived by hawking, as many people did in those days, by selling goods, mostly stolen from workplaces. He sold me a length of beautiful fabric, which, having done my pattern-making course, appeared to be of superb high quality. I did not question its source but went ahead and cut out little jackets that I intended to sell.   Later he sold me some curtain material, which I used to furnish my rural home.

One night, while we were sleeping, a burglar broke in and stole my handbag from our bedroom, but we never heard him. Fortunately, there wasn't much in it, but God revealed to me in a fresh way how the handbag would be sold by the thief. I felt convicted about this - if I bought something stolen, the owner would feel the same way as I did.   It had not occurred to me before because I had thought that if I did not know where the goods came from, then I was not doing anything wrong in buying them.   I knew then that many Christians were practising without realising that it was a sin. How did I hear that? I do not know, but I had great clarity about it.

From that day, I resolved never to buy anything from questionable sources. I started telling others that that was a sin. That is the life that I found in the city and adopted without questioning. I felt like going home and pulling off those curtains because I thought, how would I kneel and pray in a room with stolen curtains.

These were personal lessons that God taught me because He loved me and had a purpose for my life. The Bible calls the devil deceptive, and it was not long before the same hawker brought me a stunning tea set, something I had always wanted. It was hard to tell him that I could not buy it, so I said to him that I had no money. He brought it again at the end of the month, but now I felt the urge to tell him I could not buy what he was selling because I considered buying stolen goods a sin. That was the end of that, and he never brought anything to me again. The victory had been won, and God had given me boldness. It took years of pruning, but the Lord was gracious to me. He is not finished with me yet. I trust in His amazing grace. *"But you, Lord, are a compassionate and gracious God, slow to anger, abounding in love and faithfulness"* Psalm 86:15 (NIV)

In 1971, on a late September evening at Mpilo Hospital, we were blessed with our second child, a baby girl. It felt so good that we now had a boy and a girl. My husband had named our first-born, and I named our daughter Siziwe because I had found someone who was going to be my helper. There were no complications with her birth, and she was healthy and beautiful. During the Christmas holiday of that year, we went home to plough and plant in our field. The rains were good, and we produced a bumper crop of maize, groundnuts and pumpkin.

One day as I was working in the field, I was pricked by a long thorn, which went deep into the tendon in my right foot above the heel. The thorn was so stuck in that I needed help to pull it out. The pain and swelling were so bad that I could hardly walk and had to go to the hospital. It took months to heal, and I was walking on crutches.

These were times when belief in ancestral spirits was strong, so some people thought I had been bewitched because it was difficult to understand how a thorn could go that deep in that position of the foot. However, I did not entertain any talk of finding causes or remedies in *inyanga* because I had moved on in my spiritual life. I simply sought medical treatment at Mpilo Hospital and trusted God.

I must say it was very stressful. I was unable to walk for four months while Siziwe was still an infant. CJ started creche. I could not work in our fields. I can see now that even in that hardship, God was still working in me for good. My prayer and Bible reading were more regular, and as my faith grew, I found greater strength in the Lord.

We harvested eleven bags of peanuts, which we sold, and I was able to buy all the kitchenware needed for my rural home. By this time, our house in Shake was complete, so I was pleased that as expected of a young daughter-in-law, I had worked hard enough to be able to furnish my kitchen. The expectation was that a woman should work hard in the fields and produce a harvest that would bring prosperity to her home instead of relying on her husband for everything.

In 1973 I had gone back to work in the clothing factory, but I soon left because I was expecting my third child. Our second son Seluleko was born early on a Sunday morning at Pelandaba Clinic in June of that year. He was one of the first babies born in this brand-new clinic that the City of Bulawayo had built to improve health facilities in the townships. I cannot describe the joy of having a child. It did not feel like a third child, but a first son. He was not a very big baby, but he was more active, and he cried a lot, more than the first two.

It was hard to leave him at two months old to return to work, but that was all the maternity leave I had. He became an independent little boy who did not miss company much, but instead kept himself occupied. Of course, there were times when he played together with his brother despite the six-year age gap. By that time, CJ had made friends and started attending school.

A Lonely Time

I took my children to church every Sunday. My husband would help to get them ready for church and drop us off there, but he no longer attended himself. It was a lonely and trying period because our values were no longer the same. He was spending most of his free time with his friends at the beerhall and hardly saw his children. However, through all this, I did not feel that God had failed me. The Lord stood with me. In fact, it brought me more to my knees in prayer and I was ever more dependent on Him. The following scripture verse was very meaningful to me; *"When you pass through the waters; I will be with you; and through the rivers, they shall not overwhelm you; when you walk through fire, you shall not be burned, and the flame shall not consume you"* Isaiah 43:2 (ESV).

In 1974 I went to Bulawayo Technical College and advanced my pattern making skills. This two-year course was organised by the clothing industry, although it was not compulsory. It was meant to improve the skilled workers in the clothing industry, so I was offered on a part-time basis, two hours weekly in the evening. We had no car at the time but used a taxi that took me from work to college and back home, and we paid him at the end of the month. I did not regret it because I was more marketable after that. At the time, I was working at a factory in Bulawayo's Belmont industrial area, grading patterns for dresses and swimwear. Grading is the process of scaling a clothing pattern up or down in size, for instance, producing a size 10 dress pattern from a size 12 one.

At church, I sang in the choir led by Mr Isaac Mpofu. I loved the fellowship of being in the choir and singing with the congregation gave me joy. Music has always drawn me into worship and helped to lift my eyes to heaven. From the early days of singing next to my mother as a child, words from hymns have been a comfort to me and brought to mind God's promises when I have needed them most. I am very grateful to Mr and Mrs Mpofu for leading us in the choir. The Lord was still teaching me and refining me.

Help With Compulsive Behaviour

Early in my marriage, I had a sulking problem, and found it difficult to express myself if I felt hurt or offended. It would take only a minor incident for me to change from being content and happy with my husband to being silent, ill-humoured and in an offended mood. My husband, who was gentle and tender, had become accustomed to that and would leave me alone until I was ready to talk. This was a compulsive behaviour over which I had no control. It felt as if the devil had a grip on me. One day, during my devotional time, the Lord showed me how evil that was, and so I went to Jesus and asked for His cleansing. From that day on, I had such indescribable joy and freedom, it was as if my chains were broken, and I was free to love and enjoy people all the time.

I realised this truth that says, "*If we confess our sins, he is faithful and just to forgive us our sins, and to cleanse us from all unrighteousness*" 1 John 1:9 (NIV). My sins were forgiven, but there was 'unrighteousness' that I needed to be cleansed from. I praise the Lord for His mercy and goodness over my life. I was teaching Sunday school, singing in the choir, and I loved the Lord, but He saw me as I was, and I did not realise that I displeased Him. If for some reason you have one of these little things like pride, unforgiveness and other things that are in the heart which are displeasing to the Lord, you can claim 1 John 1:9. His promise is available to everyone.

In 1975 we were blessed with our fourth child, Selusiwe, our third son, born big and healthy at Pelandaba Clinic on a September evening. Even though I had experienced the joy of a new baby before, it was as sweet as it had ever felt. Our families shared our joy. I remember my father-in-law, uSeka Ferdinand, visiting us the following morning and expressing his pride in his son for having given him another grandson. This being my fourth pregnancy, and Selusiwe a quiet and contented baby, I found the early months after birth less challenging than before.

My maternity leave again felt very short, and I soon had to return to work, leaving my four young children at home. We always had a helper to assist with the children, but also had family living with us - either studying or looking for work. While a helper is important, living with family helps the children to learn to share resources and allows them to bond with family members. At various times we lived with my husband's sister Verna, brother Kenneth and my two sisters Lillian and Edna. We loved them and enjoyed their company until they moved on in life. Later, we lived with my husband's youngest brother Donald.

A Brush with Death

Two years later we were expecting again. In those days, most black people had no access to medical aid and so maternity health services, such as scans, were limited. When I had my antenatal check-ups at our local clinic in Mpopoma, the doctor thought it was one big baby because there was no scan available, and it was a normal pregnancy, so we had no concerns. I kept on wondering why I was so large in the early stages, but I had no discomfort, so I was not worried. At six months, I was still at work, but by the end of the day, my feet would be swollen, unlike during previous pregnancies. One Friday, when Ferdinand picked me up from work, I felt feverish and had a slight headache. That particular day was overcast and chilly so we thought I might have been coming down with a cold. As soon as I arrived home, I wrapped up warm and went to bed.

I woke up in the middle of the night feeling very ill, and with the worst headache, I had ever experienced. I went back to bed hoping to feel better in the morning; instead I was worse. I could not even bathe myself or walk unaided, so my husband took me to see my doctor in the city centre. My head felt as if it had been split open, and I could not move my neck backwards or forwards. We arrived to find a full waiting room at the doctor's rooms, as was usual for a Saturday, but I was called in first because my condition looked severe. She examined me, prescribed and arranged collection of medication which I took straight away, and she told me to return on the following Monday.

I spent the rest of the day in bed, and unable to eat anything or to drink. God was with me all the way. Sunday was no different, and I was increasingly fearful that even though I had taken half my medication, I was no better, and if anything felt even worse. I remembered the biblical Bartimaeus, the man whose eyes Jesus opened, and thought of his prayer in Mark 10:47, *"Jesus, Son of David, have mercy on me!" (NIV)*. God gave me the faith to believe. So I prayed, "Jesus, I am blind like Bartimaeus because I can't see what is happening in my head. I am praying his prayer". Then I continued, "Jesus, Son of David have mercy on me." After about an hour and still, in pain, I fell asleep. I woke up two hours later and found that I could move my neck with ease. When I woke up after two hours, I felt better, and my neck pain and headache had diminished. I stood up and took a bath. My body was still weak, the pain mild, and I was able to take food for the first time in two days. What a miracle! God had healed me.

I went back to work on the following day, passing by the doctors' rooms for a check-up. My doctors were twin Jewish ladies who ran a practice together. The one who had seen me was not in that morning, but when she did come in, she had asked if I had attended that morning. "Is she still alive?" She asked the nurse. I heard this from the nurse when I next visited the practice, which made me wonder why the doctor had not sent me to the hospital. I thought it was because the Lord wanted me to know Him better, that He was my Healer and that He loved me.

That prayer has been a stepping-stone for me over the years. This first-hand experience of His healing power gave me the confidence to pray for other people who are sick. I always go back and say if the Lord healed me, then He can heal anyone according to his will.

I was fit and healthy for the rest of my pregnancy, even though I decided to start my maternity leave early. When the day came for me to go to the hospital, in November 1977, I was taken

With Samu and Sibs in Mpopoma **(1978)**

by ambulance to our local clinic, where I had registered. As soon as the sister examined me, she said I had a breech baby, so she called for an ambulance to take me to Mpilo Hospital.

A Happy Surprise

When I arrived, the attending doctor said he would do a C-section, but the nurses asked him to give me a chance to deliver normally. The doctor left the room to attend to another patient but instructed them to prepare me for surgery. I started to worry, not knowing the implications of the two delivery alternatives, so I started praying that God would intervene. Sure enough, when the doctor came in the baby, Sibhekinkosi (Sibs), was on his way. Wow, they announced a baby boy! I was very pleased, praising the Lord for hearing my prayer. As he started examining me, wondering aloud why my tummy was still enlarged, he shouted, "Another baby coming!"

There was Samukele (Samu) ten minutes later! Who has any idea what that must have felt like - I was expecting a single baby by a caesarean section, but instead had two babies born naturally! O, Lord! I was carrying twins! Surely, "*If the Lord had not been on our side ... let Israel say...*" *Psalm* 124:1 *(NIV).*

All of my children, including Sibs and Samu, find it hard to believe that there was no way of knowing that I was carrying twins. Nowadays, it is unimaginable that such a thing could happen. I had prepared for one baby, and suddenly I had two. My usual preparation for each new baby had been to make two sets of matinee jackets and two wrappers in the same colour. Also, I had bought one set of a knitted jersey and some booties and a hat. A friend had given me a knitted collection of the same colour, yellow, as I had. So, in the end, I had two sets of everything, all in similar colours. When the nurses saw the clothing, they said I must have known that I was having twins, but I knew God had prepared for me in advance. He is the God of wonders who says, *"I will never leave you nor forsake you"* Hebrews 13:5b *(NKJV)*.

It was such a joy to have this wonderful gift of twins, yet equally very challenging to nurse and care for. There were no disposable nappies at the time, so we used cloth nappies that had to be washed and dried. I had three dozen of them, thinking that would be enough. Unfortunately, a week after their birth, we had a week of torrential rain and ended up with 36 wet nappies that I could not dry! That was a challenge that I will never forget. Nursing twins was unpredictable. One time they would both be up and feeding, at another one would be up and the other napping. I had to take each day as it came. It was impossible to follow a routine!

After six months, when I went back to work, we had to have two helpers looking after them. Again, the Lord was faithful to us as they were healthy most of the time, although Samu had allergy problems which were undiagnosed for many years. At two months old, she reacted with a nasty rash to a penicillin injection and had ongoing eczema until she started school at the age of five. Along with that, she had a chest problem which I was told was bronchitis, and which affected her for most of her childhood years.

Thank God again; she continued to live a normal life and enjoyed her school days. On the other hand, Sibs was a healthy and chubby baby. Wasn't it a blessing to deal with one challenge instead of two?

7

LIFE IN HARARE

I n 1979, my husband was promoted from the broadcast studio to administration, which meant a move to Harare for us. He moved first, to secure accommodation for the family, leaving Bulawayo at the end of July. His cousin, Jeckoniah Mathonsi, kindly offered him a cottage behind his main house in Mt Pleasant. The family shared meals with him, enabling him to save to buy a home in Harare. In September, it was time to say goodbye to our family and friends in Bulawayo. We had mixed feelings about the move. We had joy at being together again, but sadness at leaving all we had known and loved in Matabeleland. We were also leaving behind both sets of parents and the children, their cousins and grandparents.

My husband bought a house in the quiet suburb of Waterfalls, in the south-west of the city. It did not take us long to settle, thanks to relatives and friends who welcomed and helped us, especially Gordon Bhunu and his family, who lived just over a kilometre away. Mr and Mrs Canaan Moyo, our church-family friends, lived between the Bhunus and us. I had a pleasant surprise when I saw how much bigger our new house was. In

Mpopoma we shared a two-bedroom house between the six of us and various guests, but now we had four bedrooms.

It was on a large property, and the children had much more room to play outside. Not only that, but we also had over an acre for vegetables and seasonal crops like maize and pumpkins. Ferdinand and I had always loved growing crops, from our childhood days through to our first home in Shake, so the large field at the new house gave us much joy. We believed that the move had been guided and blessed by God and a great answer to prayer.

A New Job

At the time of our move, in 1979, I was working for the Edgars Group of stores in Bulawayo, in their factory, where they made clothing exclusively for their retail stores. I was working as a Pattern Grader with three other ladies. It was a small department, and I worked with Caroline, a Mrs Cox and Sibongile Ndiweni, Chief Ndiweni's daughter. When we arrived in Harare, our friends told us how tight the job market was. I had wondered if I would ever find a job or if I would have to return to teaching.

Amazingly, my Lord had already prepared a job for me ahead of time. There was a lady called Briar Pretorius who I had worked with in Bulawayo and who was now working at Fashion Enterprises in Harare. I just decided to call her at work, and it so happened that right at that time their company was looking for someone with my qualifications. What a wonder this was to me! God opened that door, and I was offered the job as a Pattern Grader. I praised God with Psalm 121, which has been my comfort over the years: "*I lift up my eyes to the hills. From where does my help come? My help comes from the LORD, who made heaven and earth"* Psalms 121:1-2 (ESV).

The Last-Born Arrives

Before long there was yet another cause for celebration at our home. What a double blessing! Four months after starting work, I was expecting our last child. On the 27th May 1980, our son Sitholizwe (Sitho) was born at Gomo Maternity Hospital. I spent the last month of my pregnancy in a hospital bed due to high blood pressure. After what felt like forever, he came - small but very handsome. He brought a lot of joy to my husband and me as well as to his brothers and sisters, who couldn't resist cuddling him.

From his earliest days, he showed an independent streak, such as when as a toddler he reached for a teapot on the cooker to pour himself some hot tea but spilt it on himself instead. Hilda's husband, Seka Garikai, who was living with us at the time, took him to hospital. We were all very relieved that he was not severely burnt or injured. He always insisted on doing things for himself. I look at him today and wonder where my tiny baby is. He is anything but that now!

My Journey in Prayer

When I returned to work after maternity leave, I worked for some time in my old position. Soon I was promoted to Pattern Making, which involved producing a pattern from a photo, designer sketch or finished garment. After cutting the patterns, Nicholas and Simba, my two experienced tailors would put together a sample garment. This job was more challenging, and it also brought greater financial benefits. My training from Technical College was now paying off. Nicholas, Simba and I bonded and worked well together.

One of the designers in our department was Barbara, a Jewish woman who was very humble and loving. She told me that she followed a Jewish custom in fasting every Monday. She said she did this because their family would have overeaten over the weekend, so the whole day she would just take liquids. I thought to myself, if she could discipline herself to fast for health reasons, surely, I could also fast and pray for what was important to me. By God's grace, I was able to follow through on this all day every Tuesday for the next 16 years until, for medical reasons, I could only fast for half of the day. The fitting room at work became my closet, where I prayed during every lunch hour.

I enjoy reading for leisure. From time to time, I come across the kind of book that makes an impact on my Christian walk. Once I read an article in a magazine, a true account by a woman who had come to Christ after leaving the Satanist Movement in America. She detailed the training she and others received as part of the cult. They set three to six-month prayer targets against specific young people to cause them to rebel against their parents or to take drugs and alcohol.

The Satanists stopped at nothing to destroy the young people's lives. In her story, this woman said they found it very difficult to make a breakthrough on children whose parents were praying for them. Therefore, in my everyday prayer, I mentioned all my children by name. I covered them by the blood of Jesus all the time. In the evening before we went to bed, we prayed together as a family. After everyone was asleep, I had my own quiet time because we usually had an early start in the morning.

Through these years, I continued to pray for Ferdinand, who

was still not walking with the Lord. my journey into prayer, I realised that the more I prayed, the harder the battle became but thankfully, the stronger the arm of the Lord was on my behalf. The evil one never tired of setting traps to weaken my resolve to live for my Lord.

One time, a kind and gentle work colleague approached me with a request. Gate security searched most workers as they left the factory at the end of the day. I was among those who were never searched due to our senior positions. My colleague asked if I could carry garments out of the factory for her. In return, she would give me a share of the money she would have raised from selling them. I told her that there was never a need for me to resort to that kind of life; it was not for me. If I ever needed anything, I asked my God, who met all my needs

The lady was shocked and disappointed, but I felt a sense of peace at decision and delight at being a witness for the gospel. It seemed like the same temptation that Jesus resisted from Satan in the desert, the exchange of integrity for material gain. I learnt to trust the Lord for every step I took. *"The Lord is my Shepherd; I shall not want"* Psalm 23:1 (KJV). Indeed, I soon experienced the Lord's provision.

At work, we could buy rejects - clothes which had come out with slight imperfections - for a small price. When I started working there, we only manufactured adult sizes, but as time went on, we started making clothes for both boys and girls. I felt blessed as I did not have to buy clothes at full price from retail shops, which was a great help with seven children! I only ever went shopping for school uniforms. Is He not Jehovah Jireh, our Provider!

Training Our Children

My husband was very good with our children, in particular teaching them life skills through work around the home. Every Saturday, they had chores such as washing the cars and watering the garden. Our helper was off on Sundays and had half a day on Wednesdays and Saturdays. On those days, both boys and girls shared all the kitchen work, such as cooking, doing the dishes and cleaning.

There comes a time when children, especially boys, have an urge to drive and are sometimes prepared to steal the parents' car to try it out. For many young people, this occurs at about the age of fifteen. Ferdinand avoided that temptation by sending them to driving school at the earliest opportunity, after their 'O' Levels at age 16. Years later after he died I continued this with the help of the older children who had obtained their driving licences.

My husband encouraged the children to play sport. The boys especially loved rugby and basketball and went on to play for provincial and national school teams, except Sibs who excelled at hockey and cricket, playing for Zimbabwe Schools and under 21s. On Saturdays, he was usually up early to take them to matches and training. The girls too got his support at their sporting activities such as athletics and basketball. He wanted his children around him all the time and did not encourage any of them to attend boarding schools.

I praise the Lord that my husband modelled and instilled good values and moral standards. He insisted that the children go to bed at 8:00 pm every evening so that they were refreshed and ready for school the following day. We were fairly strict about what they could or could not watch on TV, such as the soapies *Dallas* and *Dynasty*. Sometimes I listened to the children discussing how embarrassed they were at school when others were talking about what they had watched, and not knowing what had transpired. Often, they said they would wait until someone said something, then they would just say, "Yes, that was funny!" Once in a while, we would catch one of them hiding behind a sofa, trying to watch. Anyway, the instructions were clear. They always knew what they were supposed to do or not to do.

I praise the Lord that my husband was a good father. He worked diligently at his work, and it was not unusual to see him bring work home over the weekend. That way, the children learnt the beauty of working well at whatever they were called to do.

8

Church Life in Harare

When we moved to Harare, we attended Glen Norah Brethren-In-Christ Church. It was only 15 minutes away but in a high-density suburb, one of a few in Harare that black people had been restricted to before Independence. Our pastor was Rev K Q Moyo but he was soon posted to Bulawayo and his place was taken by Bingo Ncube and his wife. They were a good fit for the congregation and led us well. I taught Adult Sunday School, which I had come to love, as that combined teaching and scripture, both of which I had always loved.

The people who attended the church grew close, and soon we built what became a caring fellowship. However, as much as we enjoyed the warm church family life, we could not easily break through to the local community in outreach and evangelism. A lot of this had to do with the social and political situation at the time. During the first elections after Independence in 1980, some politicians stirred up a lot of tribal and racial tension, leading to a lot of mistrust and hatred among different ethnic groups and races. Our denomination had been established from missionary work in Matabeleland, so we often felt vulnerable as a predominantly Ndebele-speaking church in a Shona-speaking community. The atmosphere was sometimes tense but thank God the situation never went beyond that.

As a church, we continued our mandate to reach out to the lost, telling people about the love of Christ whenever we could. We started a Bible Study at our home, which Ferdinand sometimes joined. It was attended mostly by young adults such as Danisa Ndlovu, who later became the Bishop and head of the BICC, Bethuel Khumalo who played the accordion at the meetings, Charles Nyathi and Robert Mthombeni who later served as a Deacon for many years. My baking was simple, but whatever I did must have been very tasty to the young people. They started to call the Bible Study '*Woza* Friday' meaning 'Here comes Friday!' As a family, we treasure many happy memories and still share many stories and laughter from those good old days.

Seeing People as God Sees Them

When we moved to Waterfalls, most of our neighbours were white. Due to conflict before Independence and racial segregation policies under the previous regime, relationships between races were characterised by wariness and distrust. Not long after, the neighbours to our left moved away. Sadly, we had never spoken to one another, perhaps they felt they could not trust us, and we were not sure how they would respond if we had talked to them. They happened to tell us that they were selling some household goods like children's beds. When we went over to view the furniture, we discovered that they were such lovely people and they too said the same of us. I realised how easily we miss the opportunity of showing the love of Christ by being

With extended family at our first Christmas in Harare, (1980)

prejudiced or judgmental.

A new family moved in, the Matibires. We found them to be among the best neighbours that we had ever had. When they moved in, we were not at home, but they came and introduced themselves to the children. We had never had this happen to us, and it sparked an instant friendship between us, which extended to our children. We shared a lot of life with them, as well as vegetables and our harvests because they too were keen gardeners.

One Saturday afternoon, I fell ill while my husband was away. So, I just walked across to the Matibires as Mrs Matibire was a nursing sister. When I came into their house, she had just returned from work. She took my temperature and decided that she would take me to the hospital. She took me in her car, and when we arrived, I was quickly attended to, and we returned home. In the evening, before bed, she came to check on me again. What more could one ask from a loving neighbour!

The Matibires were Roman Catholic. One day Rev Holland

from BICC in Bulawayo visited our '*Woza* Friday' Bible Study, and as a form of outreach, we asked the Matibires to host it. They readily agreed and afterwards Mr Matibire was so excited. He said, "Today we really studied the Bible."

It was the first time he had ever heard the story of Jesus healing the blind young man taught. When his wife came home from work, he told her that he had dug into the Bible, relating the Bible story to her. What an opportunity to share Christ! Unfortunately, we did not continue together as we moved away soon after that.

A Difficult Situation

Meanwhile, a new pastor was appointed to our church, Rev Emmanuel Chidziva and his wife. He came at a very critical time because there was a lot of political tension. This was the time of the Gukurahundi in Matabeleland when the North-Korean trained Fifth Brigade of the Zimbabwe National Army massacred thousands of Ndebele-speaking people. Being a predominantly Ndebele church in a Shona-speaking area, we felt very unsafe. We received many threats to burn the church. Rev Chidziva was fluent in Shona and played an essential role in keeping the church safe in those days and bridging the gap between it and the community.

Around this time, Rev Holland came from Bulawayo to help us run a door-to-door outreach programme, using the Four Spiritual Laws, a short booklet presenting the gospel. We visited a few homes and the Lord was gracious to us, as they welcomed us and listened to the word. This was at the height of the ethnic tension, and our group of mainly Ndebele-speakers and a white man in Rev Holland often felt vulnerable. However, God gave

Rev Chidziva wisdom and courage, and he was able to defuse the volatile situations we encountered. Later, some of the people we had visited told Rev Chidziva that they had been moved by the love we had shown in visiting under such difficult circumstances.

A few years later, we were heartbroken when Rev Chidziva lost his wife, who passed away after a long illness. We had secured funding for her treatment from the Rotary Club, but sadly she passed away before she was able to receive it.

A Move to New Pastures

Our children were growing older, so we needed more room and started looking for another house. We had no particular preference where to move to; instead, we committed ourselves to wherever God would lead us to. Ferdinand was still not attending church and would often not join our family devotions in the evening. However, I continued to pray faithfully every evening with the children. We would say memory verses, read from the Bible, and sometimes sing and pray. I would always pray until some of them were old enough to pray themselves.

When I look back, I am amazed at how the Lord kept them interested because it was always the same pattern. They loved it even though some days it would feel like a drag, mostly when they were tired or sleepy. I inherited that from my mother. It was never an option to go to bed without prayer even after a long day or when one was feeling exhausted. My mother's favourite song, which we sang every night was, '*Othandweni LukaJesu, Sengihlala Njalo*' (In Jesus' Love, I Abide). When we were drowsy, she would sing all the verses on her own

One night I dreamt people of different races and cultures who sang in angelic voices behind me. The words of the song were:

Give me the Bible - message shining

Thy light guide me in the narrow way...

I had never heard the song before. In my dream, it was sung in isiNdebele then in English. When I shared the vision with the ladies at church, one of them happened to know the song well from the Seventh-Day Adventist hymn book. It made such an impact on me that I asked the ladies to practice it, and we sang it in church. After that, I thought no more of it.

Our house search continued in 1984, now more difficult because the building societies had run out of money for mortgages. Fortunately, our lender, Founders Building Society, would consider our application if we found a house bonded with them because they could then transfer the account. That then limited our options, but we kept on looking. One Sunday afternoon, while looking through the listings in a newspaper, we saw a house which seemed suitable.

When we looked at the map, we realised that it was about 30 km from our current home, in the northeast of the city, past the Borrowdale shops. I did not think it would be a good move, that we could never live that far from the church, work and the life we knew. It would be too expensive to drive to work every day from there. Anyway, because we had enough time on our hands, we just thought we would go and check it out.

As we drove past Helensvale shopping centre, for those of you who know the place, there are tall pine trees on one side of the road, and on the other lay the Lobels' Farm fields. Suddenly, I realised that I had seen those trees in my dream the night before, and I had also overheard someone say, "On the road to Domboshawa." I told Ferdinand that I had seen those trees in my dream the night before, but I did not know what or where Domboshawa was. He told me that we were on the road to Domboshawa!

We both liked the house, and sure enough, it was bonded by our building society. Never mind the distance, four things had come together. First, we took a liking to the house; secondly, it was bonded by our building society, third, it was priced within our range and fourth, I had been shown the road in my dream. So, I felt these things were confirmation that we had the right house.

We were excited because we had been searching for a while in vain. Unknown to us, two other couples had made offers on the house. The estate agent told Ferdinand that the owner was willing to drop the price by a thousand dollars. The next day, when my husband went to see him and finalise the deal, he asked if we wanted to take it at the asking price or less a thousand dollars. Ferdinand offered to take it as listed, which the agent accepted, saying one buyer offered to buy at the discounted price and the other's mortgage fell through.

At the very moment that Ferdinand was talking to the estate agent, I was at work on my knees as was usual at lunchtime on a Tuesday. I had no idea that he had to make that sort of decision. Come to think of it, who in their right mind would not want to buy a house at a discount? That was God. Even my husband had not known that was what the estate agent would base his decision on. So, we bought the house, which I still thought was too far from town but believed that God had led us to it.

After we moved, the distance did present challenges indeed. My work commute, which used to take 15 minutes, now took over an hour and that meant leaving home at 6:30 am and returning at 6:00 pm. We had one car, a white Peugeot station wagon, so we dropped off the kids at two different schools before I dropped my husband off at work and proceeded across the city to Fashion Enterprises. Not only that, but our church was now on the other side of the capital, an hour's drive away. Apart from the time spent driving, the cost of fuel was becoming unmanageable.

One Sunday, a few months later, we left for the church with a low reading on the fuel gauge. My oldest son, CJ, asked me if I was aware that we did not have enough fuel for the return trip. I had not realised this and said to him that God would provide. In my mind, I thought I would borrow money from someone at church. However, I had forgotten about this until someone pulled my hand as we were walking out of the church building. She put some money into my hand and told me that she was returning money that she had borrowed from me some time ago.

I had forgotten all about that loan, but the Lord was keeping it for me for that day. I praised the Lord for His provision and faithfulness, and we had enough fuel money to return home. I realised that attending church in Glen Norah was not going to be possible every Sunday, but then what? Also, I felt so lonely. I had left the many people I had got to know, friends and church family. One day, I sat down and cried to the Lord to show me why He had taken us all the way across town. I told him I was lonely, and that church was far, and I could no longer teach Sunday School.

"So, Lord, why am I here?" Did I get the answer then? No. I had to wait patiently for His time, but it was like a barren desert in my life even though I was utterly convinced that the Lord had led us there.

Around that time, we ran into our friends Shadreck and Barbara Nkala, who lived near Vainona High School, which our and some of their children attended. We had known them since high school, where Shadreck had been my classmate. Barbara suggested that our two families meet every Friday for fellowship and prayer. We readily accepted, and I was excited at the possibilities. Unlike our move to Waterfalls where we knew people from Bulawayo, there was no ready-made community in Borrowdale for our children and us. I was also looking forward to the kind of devotions, singing and prayer that I had grown up in.

We alternated, meeting at their house one week and at ours the next and continued to do this for a few months. However, our husbands did not seem to enjoy it and mostly sat and said nothing during the meetings. Furthermore, we had expected them to lead devotions and prayer, but they were not prepared to do so. So that beautiful idea died a natural death.

Attending Two Church Meetings on Sundays

Around that time, a building was going up near the Borrowdale shops which CJ said was a church, to be called Northside Community Church. Before we left Waterfalls, he had been attending a youth group at Southside Church, so he thought it was a different location of the same church. So once Northside started meeting, we let him take his younger siblings there, while I went to a new BICC group that met in the afternoon under a tree at the University of Zimbabwe (UZ) campus, about 15 minutes away. One Sunday, I brought CJ with me to the BICC meeting, under the tree. Some friends of his passed by, noticed our car, and mocked him at school the following day. Apparently, during the week the UZ grounds-staff met under the same tree for lunch and to drink *kachasu,* a homemade alcoholic brew. So, he never wanted to come with me again.

After attending a few times, I realised that Omega Nyathi from Glen Norah Church, who led the meetings was often unable to make it. So, every Sunday, I came prepared to preach in case it was required. As a result, I did most of the preaching until Rev Chidziva took over sometime later. He would preach in Glen Norah in the morning, before joining us in the afternoon. He found us a place to meet at the University Chapel, and once this happened, many university students started attending. As far as I remember, that is how Mount Pleasant BIC Church was born.

Attending Church Together

Our children were now regularly attending Northside Community Church. One day, their Sunday School teachers told the children to invite their parents to church the following Sunday to see what they were doing. My husband suggested we go with them. When we arrived, they asked the children to leave for their classes, but we never heard anything said about their parents. So, we sat through the service and listened to a good sermon from Peter Griffiths. Afterwards, we received visitors' packs and gospel tracts, and someone took down our contact details.

On the following Tuesday after work, we found visitors waiting for us at home after the children had let them in. They were David and Christine Dawanyi, who we later found out were elders at Northside. Christine had spoken to me at church on Sunday. We welcomed them, and they started chatting to us - David with Ferdinand and Christine with me. I told her that I was a committed member of the Brethren-In-Christ Church, to which she replied that since I was far from my church, I needed to be in a local church with a community around me.

I thought to myself, she does not know that I would never leave the BICC to join another denomination. This was the church and community I was born into, had grown up and been educated in, married in and had built my life within. It was a short visit, and then they left. My husband thought we should go and fellowship with them so that we could be together with the children. Anyway, for his sake and for the sake of the children I went along, but in the afternoons, I would leave them at home and meet with the group at the University.

One time, my younger sister Edna Mhlanga, came to visit from Bulawayo. She saw me going to the BIC group in the afternoon, leaving my husband and the children on their own. She thought it was not a good idea because my husband had started attending church regularly then. It felt like Moses' father-in-law giving him advice, God-given wisdom for the moment I was in. I considered it, and I stopped going to the University, only attending church at Northside with my family. I felt able to do that because by then Rev Chidziva had established himself at the UZ congregation.

Northside is an non-denominational congregation that is affiliated to the Baptist Church and is firmly rooted in the word of God. As soon as I made a decision to be there, God started showing me why He had led us to it. Firstly, our children were happy and were bonding with some of their schoolmates who also attended the church. Secondly, my husband was now regularly attending church services and midweek Bible study, even though he did not participate in the discussions. The group was split into two, to encourage his contribution, but this only slightly helped.

Marriage Enrichment Seminar

Around April 1987, the Dawanyis invited us to a weekend marriage enrichment seminar run by David and Janet Cunningham, a couple in the church. Ferdinand was sceptical, wondering what value such a weekend would have after so many years of marriage. He declined the invitation for the first of these, which were run once a year. However, the following year, he consented, and so we went.

The seminar was held at Resthaven Christian Retreat, 25 km north of Harare, and was well organised. We discovered much that we needed to change to improve our marriage. We had to make a list of what our spouse was not doing but that we had expected them to. Following that, we wrote another list, this time showing what we appreciated about each other. I was amazed at how many things we had been doing for one another without expressing appreciation for, thereby taking each other for granted.

This led to much discussion about things we had never considered, even small details such as his quiet frustration about me colour-matching his work clothes. It was such an eye-opener for both of us and simmering tensions in our marriage were entirely resolved. It is not that we had been unhappy with each other, but that we felt that our marriage was transformed for better.

On Sunday, which was the final morning of the seminar, we joyfully renewed our marriage vows, but before that, we were invited to and re-committed ourselves to the Lord. That is when it happened; after many years of not walking with God, my husband entrusted his life to Him again. I could not believe my ears when I heard him pray, asking his Father for forgiveness. My heart sang, "O Lord, you are a great and fearful God!" What more could I have asked from the Lord!

A Man Transformed

From then on, I lived with what seemed like a new man. He did not sit on the fence but crossed the line wholeheartedly. It had taken many years of prayer and fasting. I remembered once thinking to myself that I was tired of praying for him. I had given up for some years, praying occasionally, but not fervently. Then I prayed, saying,

"Lord, if I die before him, please draw him to yourself, but if he goes first, don't allow him to come to you as he is." My prayer had been answered at last, and I praised the Lord for His love and faithfulness. He now looked forward to Sunday, no longer with indifference, but expectant and joyfully. We had one car at the time, and since we could not all fit into it at the same time, he chose to take the bus.

You know when God moves; man's hand is not needed for anything. He was no longer embarrassed but would go into the bus with his big NIV Bible in his hand. All this was like a dream come true. Over the years, this experience has helped me to encourage women who are praying for their unbelieving husbands. I believe that the best prayer we can offer to God is for someone to be saved, that God delights in it. *"The Lord is not slow to fulfil his promise...but is patient toward you, not wishing that any should* perish but that all should reach repentance" 2 Pet 3:9 (ESV).I will always be grateful to David and Christine Dawanyi for their initiative and gentleness of spirit with Ferdinand. They had a heart for the lost, and the Lord used them to help him. I pray that the Lord would continue to use them to bring many into the kingdom.

I would also like to thank our small Bible study group, who always were loving and patient with my husband. We were both served and participated in every church activity that we could. The only one that Ferdinand did not take part in was the outreach ministry, Evangelism Explosion. Through the church discipleship programme, he grew steadily in his faith and was now actively engaged during Bible study meetings.

As our small group watched him grow, he was like a flower that was starting to bloom. It was beautiful to see what the Lord was doing in his life. After some time, it was as if he could not get enough of the word. After the service, he would drive across town to go to our old fellowship at Glen Norah BIC Church. He would come back and tell us how much he had enjoyed the service and the singing of hymns. I could not go with him because I had duties in the second service at Northside, which had become necessary as the church had grown. When I saw the zeal that my husband had for worshipping the Lord, I realised that the Lord had accomplished the plan He had in taking us all the way to the other side of the city. *"For my thoughts are not your thoughts, neither are your ways my ways, declares the Lord"* Isaiah 55:8 (NIV).

The Miracle Working God

CJ and Siziwe attended a church youth group that met every Friday. On their way to a meeting one evening, they picked up their friends, Tendai, the Dawanyi's son, and Elizabeth Makova. I had given them the house keys because they usually came back after 10.00pm and I would stay up to let them in. While I was preparing for bed, we suddenly heard a desperate

Our home group at Northside Community Church (1990)

knock at the door. My husband rushed to open it to David Dawanyi, with the news that our children had been involved in a road accident. Listening from the bedroom, I could hear my husband asking, "Where? Are they all right?"

Many thoughts went through my head about what might have happened, and I feared the worst. They had been driving along Borrowdale Road, on their way from church and not far from the Dawanyis. Slowing down to take a turn, they were hit from behind by an enormous army truck, which later we discovered was driven by a drunk driver. Their Mini Cooper spun and rolled into the long grass beside the road but thank God it landed on its wheels. In the next moment, a second army truck approaching from the opposite direction and collided with the first one, knotting the two together. From the impact, the top of one of the trucks flew off, throwing a soldier out onto the road. Sadly, he did not survive, dying the instant he hit the tarmac. Most of the passengers from both trucks sustained severe injuries. A life was lost unnecessarily due to drinking and driving.

CJ and Tendai only needed a few stitches on their foreheads, and Siziwe had a concussion. Elizabeth sustained a slightly worse injury because she fell out of the car through the broken window of the Mini. That had been our only car at the time, so we had to walk to the location, which was only 10 minutes away, but it felt like the longest we had ever taken.

As we approached the scene having walked from home in fearful silence, we could see the debris; two truck batteries on the road, a diesel spill and many bits and pieces of metal. I felt a sense of horror when I saw a body on the road covered with a red blanket. I feared that one of our children was lying under it. It feels almost as fresh in my mind now as it did then. We arrived to find that David had already rushed the boys to the hospital, while Christine had transported the girls.

We received a lift to the hospital, and on arrival, the boys were waiting for us, but we were not allowed to see the girls. We feared the worst, thinking that perhaps their injuries were worse than we had thought. We were able to see them after an hour's wait, and thankfully, they were not as bad as we had imagined. This incident helped me to realise how much, just every moment, our lives are in God's hands. One second later would have seen our children sandwiched between those two trucks, which took a whole day to untangle.

The incident had an impact in the community. For example, a woman whose house faced the scene of the accident visited to say she believed only God could have rescued them, and because our children had been returning from church, He had acted to

protect His people. The officer who took the statement had asked CJ where they had been coming from. When CJ
told him, the officer said, "You must worship and hold onto your
God because you guys were saved miraculously."

God took them out of harm's way just at the right moment,
and we praised Him for His faithfulness. The Lord
had snatched them out of the lion's mouth.

9

Back to Bulawayo and Illness

On Monday evenings at Northside Community Church, an intercessory prayer group would meet to pray for the church. Sometime in 1989, the group said to the leadership that as they prayed, they saw a picture of the church as a broken vase, and they sensed God calling our congregation to more fervent prayer. In response, the elders decided that all leaders and volunteers would travel to Resthaven Christian Retreat for prayer and fasting one Saturday a month. We would start the day together with praise and a devotion, after which we went out to seek the Lord in individual prayer.

It was during one of these moments of solitary prayer, in early January 1990, that I sensed the Lord prompting me to ask the intercessory group to pray for my family. While I was praying, God laid this scripture on my heart: "*For I know the plans I have for you, plans to prosper you and not to harm you, plans to give you hope and a future" Jeremiah 29:11 (NIV).* So, I wrote it down, but I battled the rest of the day's retreat, and the whole day on Sunday because I was not sure whether I was hearing from God or was it just my thinking. Eventually, I decided to tell the intercessory group in case it was God's voice that I had heard. Later, at the evening service, I shared my burden with the leader of the group despite the doubts that beset me. What caused me to doubt was that everything was going well, and the children were flourishing in and outside of school. What I forgot was that God knows the future that lies beyond the present that we see.

A Sudden and Unexpected Turn

The intercessors took the request seriously, praying for my family when they met on the following day. Two weeks later, the earth suddenly fell beneath our feet. Ferdinand was doing well at work when he received the bombshell news that he had to immediately move to Bulawayo, to head up the ZBC in Montrose.

He had done well since we arrived in Harare, having been promoted from a broadcaster at Mbare Studios to Director of Personnel for ZBC at their Borrowdale headquarters. However, this was a time when the government was consolidating its control over the national broadcaster, replacing professionals with political appointees. Ferdinand was one of the three directors replaced. At the same time, the other two were forced to retire while a post was created for him in Bulawayo.

The Director-General told him that he would be travelling abroad for two weeks and expected him to have moved to Bulawayo by the time he returned. Ferdinand tried to reason with the Director-General, saying two weeks was not enough time to hand over to his replacement, but the DG insisted, "When I return, you must be in Bulawayo. Am I making myself clear?"

"What about accommodation?" Ferdinand asked.

With Ferdinand, receiving a farewell present from our
homegroup when leaving Harare **(1990)**

"Well, try and make arrangements for a second mortgage if
you need one. The point is you have to move, whatever it takes."

This was difficult news to break to the children, who had
grown up in and were settled in Harare. They were thriving at
school, plugged-in at church and had made close friends in our
neighbourhood. We prayed about the move and began to feel the
peace of God about it. At least, we thought, we would be close to
the rest of the family. However, we continued to pray for wisdom to make the right decisions, especially involving the house.

Now it was apparent that that word of prayer had come from
the Lord. But praise the Lord, we knew the intercessory prayer
group had already covered us. We considered whether to rent out
or to sell the house. After taking advice from friends, he decided that the right thing to do was to sell it and buy one in Bu-

lawayo. We had to do this quickly because it was only two weeks into the new school year and for Samu & Sibs, the start of High School. Unlike the preceding years where we could only afford to buy summer uniforms, this time we had bought everything, including blazers and tracksuits for winter. Who would buy these uniforms from us? How would we be able to purchase new uniforms, books and kit for the new schools?

Well, the starting point was for Ferdinand to go ahead while I stayed with the children to complete their first term of school. Meanwhile, he would be looking for school places for children in Bulawayo once we knew where we would live. Seluleko was already registered to sit his 'O' levels that year at Vainona High so he could not move elsewhere. Thankfully, my sister Elsa and her husband Leonard Masuku had recently relocated to Harare, living close to his school. We asked them to take him in, and they kindly agreed. Praise God, that part was sorted.

CJ was already working, he had to decide whether to go to Bulawayo and lose his job or stay in Harare. He chose to stay, but this meant finding new accommodation since he had been living at home. We requested our family friends, the Ndimandes, if they would kindly let him stay at their cottage, which they did. One by one, the pieces of the puzzle were being fitted together.

Meanwhile, Ferdinand moved to Bulawayo, staying with my sister Edna and her husband Tinos Mhlanga, and got on with the task of buying a house. In Harare, I tried to sell our home, go to work, and pack for the move. It was not an easy time as the children were still attending school, and we had to keep the house ready for viewing by potential buyers. I was working full time at the Church, having left my job at Fashion Enterprises the previous year. I travelled to Bulawayo a few times to view properties with Ferdinand. It was not a good time to be looking as there were only a few available.

One day, after visiting a few houses and not finding anything suitable, we sat down in desperation and prayed that God would lead us to the right home. The house that we eventually bought, in Matshemhlophe, was actually the first house that we had viewed but thought we would find something better. After two weeks of searching, we went back to it. You will hear later why God led us to that house.

Once we bought the house, finding school places was the next challenge. It was challenging to get spots in the schools we preferred as classes had been filled at the start of the year. Some of the children had to drop subjects that they had been studying in Harare. My husband went from school to school, trying to get suitable places. With all that, we kept coming back to the Lord in prayer, reminding ourselves that the prayer group had already brought all these things before Him. At the end of the first term in April, we all moved to Bulawayo after ten years in Harare.

It felt like moving to a new Bulawayo, which had changed much since we left before Independence. Communities that we had lived in had changed as many Black families had moved across the city into suburbs from which they had previously been prohibited. For the children, it was a fresh start as they had no memory of the friends they had made when we had lived in Bulawayo. In a way, it was more straightforward because they did not try to look for anyone but made friends with the people they met.

We soon had to make an important decision about where to fellowship. Our old church, BICC Mpopoma, was now too far from our new home. Also, many of the people we had fellowshipped with 10 years previously had moved, mostly to Bulawayo Central Church as they moved houses across the city. This was now our nearest congregation too, so it became our home church. It was led by Daryl Climanhaga, whose father David had served the church as Bishop for many years before retiring to the USA.

Coming from Northside, we found it very different and had difficulty fitting in. We had become used to a multicultural church community, less formal service and worship style, and involvement in church ministries, which is not what we found in Bulawayo. We did our best to adjust, and over time helped to start a Bible study, prayer meeting and coordinated a marriage weekend at Shalom Campsite. At the time, Church met in the Anglican Church building near the City Hall, but soon relocated to the Baptist Church, in preparation for a move to their own new building.

Leadership Training at Haggai Institute in Singapore

Not long after we moved to Bulawayo, God had opened a way for me to travel to Singapore for women's leadership training at the Haggai Institute. The Institute covered the cost of my trip and Northside Community Church generously paid my US$300 registration fee. This was the first time I had travelled in an aeroplane, so I was both excited and apprehensive, not knowing what to expect. Our first flight took off from Harare early on a bright, sunny morning. I sat next to Mrs Aggrinah Kaliyati, who had flown many times before and who was the only other Zimbabwean attending the course. She was chatting away and did not realise how terrified I felt, and much more so as the plane flew higher and higher. Later, I adjusted and felt settled. It took three flights to reach Singapore, so it was a blessing to be with someone who had experienced international travel.

When we arrived, we were roomed separately to help us experience different cultures and languages. I shared a room with a lady from Sierra Leone, and we developed a good friendship. If I remember correctly, there were 45 of us from thirty-three Third World countries. The aim of the training was to equip men and women from less developed countries who would go back and train their own people in leadership. Sessions were held separately for men and women. There were two of us from Bulawayo, Aggrinah, who was a nursing sister at Mater Dei and I. We had a fantastic time together and developed a friendship over the month that we were there.

One of the things that really touched me there was to see Indian women who loved reading the Bible. They were so committed to the Lord. I knew that BICC had churches in India, but among the Indian community in Zimbabwe, I had never seen a single Christian. Most of the population of Singapore is of Chinese, Malay and Indian heritage. It was a blessing to be able to attend church services and receive such a warm welcome. We appreciated that even though they had their own languages, they held services in English to accommodate different nations. This made me alive to the potential for the church in Zimbabwe to reach all racial and language groups.

An Act of Kindness

Singapore is both the name of an island and of the beautiful city that is built upon it. It is a spotless city, we were told that littering would result in a fine of US$10, so everybody became cautious about tidiness. One time, after we had finished our lessons for the day, Mrs Kaliyati and I travelled across the city to the Singer sewing machine shop to look for one for myself. I was successful in finding one, but unfortunately, we could not find our way back.

We flagged down a taxi and asked the driver to take us back to the Haggai Institute. He accepted, we got in, and he drove off. After driving for some time, he brought us back to the spot he had picked us up from, indicating he did not know where our destination was. He did not understand English, but he collected his fare and let us know that he could not help us in any way. We were desperate because shops were about to close, and we had no idea how to return to the Institute. Just then, a young man, who looked like he was in his teens, came to us and said, "Can I help you?"

"O, yes, please!" we replied. Mrs Kaliyati gave him an envelope with the Institute's phone number. He called the place, and they gave him directions. He offered to take us there, in his car we assumed. But we were surprised to see him board a bus with us and show us our stop when we arrived there. O yes, God really sent an angel to guide us back to the Institute.

One of the stories that touched me was told by an Indian lady who said that right at the southern tip of India, Christian churches were established because someone had stuck a gospel tract in her family's thatched roof. Many years later, when it was re-thatched, her father found it. He secretly read it, became a Christian and shared the good news with his family. They too were saved, a church was born in their house, and several congregations had since grown from there. What a testimony to the importance of tracts! We need to give them out, and any other Christian literature, as we never know who the Lord will bring into the kingdom.

It was an incredible privilege to attend the leadership training, which equipped me for ministry in various aspects within the church, especially in women and children's work. We took notes and were given handouts, which have guided me over the years, as well as helped me to train others. I am deeply grateful to God and to those who donated to the Haggai Institute to afford me and many others this opportunity. I am also thankful to Northside Church for their contribution without which I would have been unable to attend.

Ferdinand Falls Ill

I was happy to be back home a month later, but I was met with the news that Ferdinand was not feeling any better, but much worse instead. Before I left for Singapore, he had been complaining of back pain and frequent headaches. He had kept his worsening condition from me while I was away, so as to not trouble me. However, he continued going to work, even though he would sometimes experience blackouts. The property that we had bought needed a lot of work, including fencing the boundary and paving the driveway. Praise the Lord, we were able to build a wall along the front length of the property and do other work as well because we had paid off the mortgage.

Ferdinand had been seeing his General Practitioner (GP) who had not realised how serious his ailment was. By then, he was having blackouts at the same time of the day at about 10 am without fail. He would go to work, and at the said time, he would have to lie down in their sickbay. I became increasingly frustrated with his GP's lack of urgency in the face of his significant symptoms. One day, I called her, stressing his symptoms and insisted she refers him to a specialist.

She did so, later that same day. She made an appointment with a Dr Cohen. The specialist then checked his vital organs such as the heart, kidneys, and liver and could not find anything wrong. In my prayers, I went to God each time with the promise He had given me from Jeremiah 29:11, "*For I know the plans I have for you, declares the Lord, plans to prosper you and not to harm, plans to give you hope and a future*" (NIV).

"Lord, how can this promise be true when my husband is in this condition?" It was difficult to reconcile God's love for us with the suffering that he was allowing Ferdinand to experience. But who can ever know the mind of God?

My father-in-law, who was not a Christian at the time, expressed his desire to take his son to traditional healers. I remember the conversation that we had with him in our living room in Matsheumhlope. While in our hearts we said, "No!", I tried to be respectful and diplomatic in declining his offer. I politely told him that if we did that, we would be drawn backwards spiritually, to where we had come from. I did not believe that my father-in-law would listen or budge, but I know many people must have been praying for us because he did listen and honour our wishes. Traditionally, I would really have no say in that, he would have just called his other sons and gone ahead with the plan. I marvelled at his response because it was so unlike him to take into account other people's views. Was this not more evidence of the Lord's promises to us in Jeremiah 29:11 coming to pass? Plans to prosper us and to give us a future.

The devil was still trying to find ways of getting to us because some of my husband's friends would call him while I was at work offering to take him to Guta Ra Mwari, a cult that claimed to be a church with healing powers but worshipped a man whom they called Simo, meaning The Image (of God). We would not have accepted a visit from this kind of church that incorporates traditional beliefs but had agreed between us that anyone who wanted to come and pray with us would be welcome, but we were not going to go anywhere to look for someone to pray for us. We felt the presence of God when we prayed at home, so we did not believe that He would be more powerful elsewhere. Therefore, when his friends called, he told them that he would discuss it with me first. That would be the end of the conversation because they knew that he did not want to go. They also knew I would not to budge.

We just took one day at a time, even though we did not understand God's plans. At first, his headaches lasted from midnight till morning, but gradually they persisted all night. His cousin Regina recommended that we see Dr Omara, a specialist physician. This doctor said Ferdinand's head had a lot of pressure and hospitalised him to urgently carry out various tests.

After two days, he sent him to Harare for a PET scan, which is a test where radioactive dyes are introduced into the body, after which an image is taken by a machine, allowing the doctor to check for abnormalities. Dr Omara said we should not drive but fly and return on the same day. I am ever so grateful for family and friends who paid for our flights. These are Jeconia Mathonsi, Daniel Ndlela and Gordon Bhunu.

When Dr Omara received the results, he told us that Ferdinand had a brain tumour the size of a tennis ball. He said it was pressing on his brain, which explained the blackouts, and why he sometimes experienced temporary blindness. He then referred him to a neurologist, Mr Kalangu. Without delay, in November 1990, Ferdinand was admitted to Mater Dei Hospital for surgery. After surgery, my husband would just say to me, "Pray for me."

As expected, family and friends flocked to see him, until the surgeon told me to ask people not to visit so he could get time to heal. During the night after the surgery, the nursing sister who was attending my husband in ICU said he had prayed a wonderful prayer, even though when we visited, he could hardly speak. She said she had written the prayer on a piece of paper, which she had misplaced.

After a week, Dr Kalangu asked to see me, and I had no clue what he might say. I had thought that the surgery had been successful, that Ferdinand would recuperate and be well again. In any case, I felt that if it had been something serious, he would have asked me to bring someone. But yes, Dr Kalangu had bad news for me. He told me that my husband had a malignant tumour. Spontaneously, without much thought, I asked him, "How much time does he have left to live? Can we take him somewhere else for treatment, maybe outside the country?"

"I am sorry Mrs Sibanda, you cannot take him anywhere or outside the country. Even if you do, there is nothing more that can be done other than what I shall do. I want to reassure you that I am going to do all I can to help him. And I really cannot say how much time he has."

Indeed, throughout my husband's illness Dr Kalangu did all he could. He even gave us his home number so that we could call him at any time. In the end, he was like family to us. He was a remarkable doctor, and I will never forget him.

Before my husband had gone for surgery, Seluleko's 'O' Level Cambridge results had been released, and he had done very well. In the previous year, before we moved from Harare, he had asked if we would send him to St Georges, a prestigious private school, where some of his friends had transferred to. For admission to 'A' Level study the college required at least 5 A's at 'O' Level and his father had said if he met the requirements, then he would go to boarding school at St Georges. He had qualified and had been offered a place.

Unfortunately, due to the situation we found ourselves in, it would be difficult for him to go to Harare while the whole family was in Bulawayo and with his father in that condition. I found it hard to disappoint him at that stage as I did not know what future we were facing. But my husband was very adamant that he needed to go and get a transfer letter to Christian Brothers College nearby.

"NaSja," as he called me, "someone told me in a dream not to send my son to St Georges. He said you would have problems with his fees when I am gone. But I was assured that he would become a graduate still." That shocked me, and I did not know how to take it. Anyway, Selu went to Harare and obtained a transfer letter, and started his A-Levels at Christian Brothers College (CBC).

There it was. Dr Kalangu had confirmed my fears. I was faced with a new reality which I did not know how to handle. I was devastated, and the future had suddenly looked desolate ahead of me. I broke down then. As Dr Kalangu walked out, Mrs Kaliyati came in to be with me and comfort me. O how much I appreciated her! Remember, we had only recently returned from Singapore together. Had the Lord been preparing us for this time? I don't know.

Meanwhile, Mrs Kaliyati had called home for CJ to

bring Ferdinand's parents, who were staying with us in Mat-sheumhlophe at the time. As I left the hospital, they were coming in. I did not know how to face them with the devastating news. Neither did I know how to tell our children, and my husband since at the time, he was still unwell in ICU. At home, I was overwhelmed by the news. My mother-in-law arrived, and we cried together. She said to me, "NaSja, be strong! Do not bring him down sooner than he is meant to." I had to pull myself together, as I did not have enough time to sit and cry. I needed to go and help him at the hospital. The news devastated our children, families and friends. It was an utterly terrible time in my life, though it felt like a horrible dream that would pass. We were covered by prayer from family, from the Church family and the many friends who stood with us.

As the days went by, he seemed to get better and was able to talk to people. However, his right hand and foot were paralysed, but the doctor said that this would improve with time. He started physiotherapy at the hospital. A month later, on Christmas eve, the doctor said we could take him home, but if we could not manage to keep him comfortable in his state, we could take him back to the hospital.

Ferdinand was very excited to be home with the children after some time at the hospital, so much that he did much better at home than he had at Mater Dei. The days settled into a routine of taking him to Mater Dei for physiotherapy in the morning, home for lunch, then driving across town to Mpilo Hospital for radiotherapy. He had improved and was able to walk with a cane, but in February, he lost feeling in both legs, so he was in a wheelchair until he was called home.

However, I never lost hope in God and prayed and fasted for

him to be well again. We had continued our evening devotions with the children, but each day Ferdinand and I had our own prayer and devotional time, discussing scripture and following the 'Our Daily Bread' booklet. Each time he prayed I could not believe that he was the same man that I had known. He was full of faith and trust in God. That is where we got our strength from; those prayer times were our powerhouse.

Ferdinand had a heart for his brothers to be saved. They were living the life that he used to live, but now that he had a relationship with the Lord, he wanted the same for them. When we had two cars, before my husband had surgery, on Sunday mornings, he would go ahead of us to pick up his brother and his family from Sauerstown.

One morning, he was feeling unwell, but he went to collect them and finding that they were not ready, he sat in the house and fell fast asleep. They must have thought that he needed to rest, so they let him sleep until it was too late for the service. He was disappointed because he was expecting them to wake him up. I think that was the last time he was able to pick them up because he became weaker and weaker after that. But he asked me to pray for them.

"Please pray for my brothers and father to be saved." I am pleased that the brother he used to go and pick up found the Lord before he too passed away. So did my father-in-law, who had an encounter with the Lord on his death bed.

After my husband's surgery, the ZBC Director-General who had transferred him to Bulawayo called and asked if he could come to Harare and help in his previous office, which had become dysfunctional since his departure. His boss was not aware of how severe his condition was because there was no way Ferdinand would have the energy to do that. However, the staff at Montrose Studios were of invaluable support to us because they provided transport and a driver for all the hospital runs, for physiotherapy and radiotherapy. Finally, when they decided to retire him on the grounds of illness, they invited us to ZBC Bulawayo for a small ceremony. Over and above his benefits, they gave him a car, a Nissan Pulsar. We were grateful because it was still in decent condition and we still had a lot of running around to do. At the time, we had a Peugeot station wagon, which was expensive to maintain and run.

I will never forget the help that we received from Island Hospice. They provided us with all the equipment we needed to make my husband as comfortable as possible. We appreciated their weekly visits to support and encourage us. There was Daphne, and Joyce Kandarira, ever so loving and helpful. We had sourced a nurse aid to help during the day, which allowed me to go to work half-day and to do the school runs. At the time I did office administration work at Evangelism Explosion III. There were several nurse aids that we used, but there was one who stayed with us until the end. Her name was MaZulu. She had great compassion for her patient and did everything she could to ensure his comfort.

Together, with our helper who did the garden, they made an excellent team. One day, my husband said he wished to give them each some cash to buy a goat that they would keep and use it for their future. After he died, I was proud to fulfil his wish and gave them each enough money to buy a goat. They loved him because he was an easy and happy patient since he had a living hope in his Saviour Jesus Christ.

Even though we had a nurse aid and gardener to help, the

children still had many responsibilities. In the evenings, they helped me to lift Ferdinand into his wheelchair and bed. They did this readily without hesitation, even when it was exam time. The last born Sitho, aged 11 and too small to lift his father, would lift Ferdinand's feet onto the wheelchair footrests. With that, he was content to have helped his father. It was a tremendous privilege for the children and me to be able to care for him at home, which was far better than him being in the hospital.

All our evenings spent around the living room where Ferdinand sat; having meals, fellowship and evening prayer together. This was God's amazing grace because, in the hospital, they would not have been able to spend time with him. Those are some of the things one might take for granted, but I do realise that it was a blessing.

God is always sovereign. As time drew close for him to go, we just watched the hours of the night go by from the clock that was hanging on our bedroom wall. He would sleep up to midnight and then after that he would be up and fall asleep again at 5am in the morning.

For me, it would be time to get up to get the children ready for school. I remember him saying he had cried, so I asked why he did because we had agreed that we were not going to be depressed, but we were going to draw strength from each other. He said it was because I worked during the day and spent the night awake with him. I felt that maybe he had cried to God that He would give us both some good rest.

His Will be Done?

I was thinking about all that as I was driving from town once. I seemed to hear God say to me, "Am I not allowed to do what I want to do with the person that I brought into this world?" With tears running down my face, I said, "Lord, your will be done!" I had never been able to pray that God's will be done before. I had been afraid to pray those words.

The first reason was that it would have felt like giving up, surrendering my belief that God could fully heal him, however bleak the outlook was. Secondly, I was afraid that if God's will was to take my husband, then in my praying for His will to be done I would be praying for my husband to be taken from me. I was not ready to face that reality. I learned later that as sincere as my prayer for healing was, it was not God's will to let him live.

Looking back, I praise the Lord that even though it was distressing to see my husband paralysed, it was a relief that he did not experience the agony that cancer can cause. I was surprised that some people from church would come to me saying even though I was a Christian, I should not neglect the traditional healers and ancestors. I had expected that fellow Christians to encourage me to be unwavering in my faith at the moment of my greatest need.

I praise the Lord that Ferdinand was saved, or else it would have been difficult to stand against the many arrows that the devil threw at us. The victory was close, but so hot was the battle. One of his relatives visited and said, "There is someone who prays for the sick. Are you willing for him to come here and pray?" We did not understand what kind of faith healer this was, but it was clear to us that he would not be the kind of person that we would have wanted. My husband said to this relative, "Please leave me alone! You are interfering with my faith." This was the final blow that the devil received. There was no other chance because soon it was time for him to go.

The Final Goodbye

Two weeks later, on a Tuesday evening, our evening devotional included a text on Jesus Christ's return with focus on verse 16; *"For the Lord himself will descend from heaven with a cry of command, with the voice of an archangel, and with the sound of the trumpet of God. And the dead in Christ will rise first"* 1 Thessalonians 4:16 (ESV).

He had a glow on his face as he read this and had a sense of hope and peace in him. It had been the usual evening until supper, where he had the fish he had asked for. He became ill, and his breathing was laboured throughout the night. He needed two fans going throughout the night to keep him cool but then settled a bit early in the morning. Before the children went to school, I asked them to go and say goodbye to him. I remember Sibs telling him that he had come 8th in class. I called CJ in Harare and members of the family to tell them that things had changed. His youngest brother Donald came, and Ferdinand said to him that he was going that day.

The nursing sister from Island Hospice arrived for the routine check-up. She said that his pulse was low and advised that we call a Minister. I thought she believed that maybe Ferdinand should be given the last rites as they do in some Churches, but that is not the practice at BIC Church. Ferdinand thought it unnecessary, but she insisted, and we called the Bishop's office but he, along with the other ministers were out, attending his grandchild's funeral. My husband smiled at me, such a smile that has stayed with me.

Before the Sister left, she told my mother-in-law that her son had only thirty minutes to live. Later I wondered why she had not said that to me as well because I only heard about it later after he had gone. Anyway, at about half-past ten, he asked for milk, not in a cup as usual but in the small measurement that he used to take his morphine. After taking that milk, he fell asleep for about ten minutes. I also fell asleep leaning on his bed. When he woke up, he wanted us to make him sit in the wheelchair, but I said we would pull him up on the bed instead because whenever he sat up, his breathing became more laboured. As soon as we put his feet on the floor, he said he was dizzy and wanted to lie down.

As we were laying him down on that Wednesday, 23rd October 1991, he went to sleep in the Lord. He had just turned 51 years on 23rd September. What finality death brings. One minute we were talking to him, the next there was no answer from him, and he was gone. The long battle with cancer was over.

All the children were still at school. Only Samu was in the house at the time. I felt very sorry for her because she had only heard me crying and nobody had remembered to tell her. Later, I remembered that she was there. I went in, hugged her and said to her that her dad was gone. When death comes suddenly, it is as if people were not prepared. My father-in-law who was already there, and Ferdinand's brother Earnest who arrived minutes after he died, took care of everything that was supposed to be done. It was God's providence that they were there because it would have been challenging for my mother-in-law and myself to do it ourselves.

It was hard to see the children return from school to a fatherless home. I was more heartbroken for my children than I was for myself. Preparations for the funeral went on as happens in our culture. Traditionally, my place was to grieve surrounded by women from family and friends, so I had no idea about any arrangements made except to answer any questions I was asked. His dear family and friends from Harare; Jeckonia Mathonsi, Gordon Bhunu and Daniel Ndlela bought him a lovely coffin. I am very grateful to God for these lifelong friends that showed their love to the end.

My husband was laid to rest on Saturday, 26th October at Athlone Cemetery. The support from family, friends, church family, as well as loving people of Bulawayo as a whole was remarkable. Nicknamed *uGodogodo Olungahlalwa Yinyoni*, he was well known across the city, having been a radio broadcaster for some years. I was grateful that Mrs Victoria Chitepo, then Minister of Information under whose responsibility the ZBC operated; was a down to earth person. Having been widowed herself, she was a source of comfort to me.

ZBC worked hard, and I am very grateful to people like Mrs Abbie Dube, who was at the forefront of the team. She came not only as a work colleague, but she is my husband's aunt. I was comforted by the support of Northside Community Church, who sent Pastor Ian Wilshire and Mrs Christine Dawanyi to represent them. I will not be able to mention everyone by name, but the funeral was a success and a fitting farewell to him. We appreciated a poem that was written and read by Barbara Nkala, who came all the way from Harare. Thank you, MaMthunzi.

After the Funeral

After everything had been done and even the relatives who had remained had left one by one, I had only my mother-in-law and her sister Naka Rifford stayed behind to keep me company. They were praying women who gave me so much comfort. It was customary in those days that if a husband died, his widow would wear a black dress and head-covering for a year, at the end of which it would be replaced with a new dress that his family would buy.

Naka Rifford took me to the garden and put the dress over me, according to custom. In my heart, I said, "Lord, I receive this dress. It is a gift like any other that you have given me." By this, I meant that I was accepting His will, new name and identity as a widow, and this dress as a symbol of it. I am pleased that this custom is fading away slowly. It was depressing for me, as anyone who has worn it understands, because when I was among other people, I always drew attention.

To mark the end of this period, a ceremony took place and included the distribution of his clothes and personal possessions. My father-in-law said because there were sons in the home, they could take what they wanted and the rest I would do whatever I wanted to do with it. When the boys had picked up what they wanted, which was for sentimental purposes, I gave away most of the clothes to my father-in-law and his clan. From that day, I realised that the possessions that we so value in the world are nothing without Christ.

When relatives and friends were still around, the loss of my husband did not seem real. The house was full of people, its contents re-arranged to accommodate and cater for all the mourners, so it did not feel like home. But when life returned to normal and the furniture was back in its place, the reality and finality of his death settled on me. The empty seat he used to sit on, the medicine dispenser he had used, and his Bible were all agonising reminders that Ferdinand had gone.

Grieving Together as a Family

Before the funeral, I did not get the opportunity to spend any time with my children. The older ones were at home, but I was surrounded by women who mourned with me right until the funeral so I could not speak to them. The younger ones were at my uncle's home, Mr and Mrs J D Ndlovu. This was so that children would not be distressed by all the mourning, and to ensure that their daily needs were cared for. So, Sibs, Samu and Sitho had been away, and now everyone was back in the same house. At first, it was awkward, we were all grieving privately but did not know what to say to each other. God gave me wisdom, and I spoke to them individually, asking them what they had found most painful about Ferdinand's death and funeral. I do not remember everything they said, but some said the church had been the worst for them, and the youngest said,

"When they were putting dirt on my father". Piercing words! This triggered more open conversation, and slowly they were able to talk, even about his illness and funeral. My children expressing themselves about anything that came to their minds helped us to start healing and working through our grief.

As for me, I had a lot to process. There had obviously been a routine with regards to meals, bathing, and medication. Suddenly, I did not have all that to do. How would I start life? I was still at home, had not returned to work and battled with my thoughts. Strangely, I missed that routine but was comforted by the thought that my husband was no longer experiencing the suffering that made it necessary. I replayed in my mind all that had happened from the start of his illness to his death, and how and where things could have been different. Every time, however, my thoughts would lead me to say that 'God is merciful' because, despite the loss, I saw His mercy and provision in all that had happened. He understood me even better than I did understand myself.

A Conversation with God

Ferdinand and I had been having our quiet time, reading scripture and praying together. But when I tried to do that by myself, there was no inspiration. Nothing. For two weeks, I would kneel down, try to pray, but found myself running out of words. I prayed;

"Lord, why is this happening? You are not finished with me." It was amazing that I heard from God there while I was on my knees. The Lord said two things to me:

1. Remember I could have taken him before surgery, a year ago before you did not even know how to sign a cheque?

2. Remember, you asked for three things and I granted them to you? "Yes, Lord!" I said as I remembered all the times, I had made these requests in my prayer. These were the things that I had asked for:

"Lord if anything happens to my husband, I want to be there with him" This was granted.

"Lord, please don't allow him to go back to the hospital again." At the time he needed to be turned on his side every 30 minutes, which the hospital staff hadn't time to do. God granted me this.

"Lord, please don't take the use of his arms." (Because paralysis was moving up his body and his doctor had told me that if it moves further, he would lose the use of his arms. At least he could still feed himself and brush his teeth). That too was

granted.

I wept and asked for forgiveness from God. He had seen my heart, and I had not shown gratitude to him. I honestly did not realise that my emotions were standing between a Holy God and me. I thought I had accepted that it had been His will to take my husband, but I had not fully done so. He is God; He searches our thoughts, motives and emotions.

From then on, I began to appreciate many things that I had not realised before. I never looked back even though I still had much grieving to live through. Instead, I began to appreciate Him and be thankful to Him for the doctors and the nurses that were loving and helpful, and for everyone that He had called to pray for us. He says, *"I the Lord search the heart and examine the mind,"* Jeremiah 17:10 (NIV).

God is full of mercy and compassion. He allows us to question Him and to doubt Him, but gently He restores a proper sense of perspective in us.

Days of Loneliness

My devotions and prayer times started again, and I enjoyed going to God every day. Somehow, Friday evenings were the worst days for me as we had always enjoyed each other's company at the end of the work week together. I felt lonely and really missed my husband. The comfort that he had died in the Lord with the hope of glory was my greatest comfort, but nothing could replace his presence.

One Friday evening, feeling desperate, I prayed and said, "Lord Jesus, I have no one to turn to. I will be your friend. I will tell you everything. Please be my friend." Secondly, I asked that He should not give me another husband but help me to bring up my children in a godly way. With five boys and two girls, aged 11 to 24ys, I was overwhelmed. How would I be able to bring them up to fear God?

He gave me Psalm 68:5 *"A father to the fatherless, a defender of widows, is God in his holy dwelling" (NIV)*.I read this scripture to them to encourage them and show them that even though their earthly father had gone, their heavenly father would always be there. I explained that their father and I sometimes struggled to get things for them, but our FATHER in heaven will not lack anything. It was a verse that I too needed to hear; to know that He had been with me as a child, as a single woman, as a wife and mother, and even now as a widow. He would undoubtedly take care of me.

Things Fall into Place

I looked back at the time when the Lord told me to ask the intercessors to pray for my family back in 1989, and I realised how things had fallen into place.

First, when we sold the house in Harare and bought one in Bulawayo, we paid cash for it so that I was left without a mortgage. That was a considerable expense taken off my budget. Not only that, but there was money left over to enable us to do the necessary work on our new property.

Secondly, the house was a stone's throw away from Christian Brothers College, where the four boys attended school, so they walked, and I didn't have to drop or pick them up after school.

Third, having all the extended family around at the time of the bereavement was a great comfort. If we had still been in Harare, it would have been very challenging for them to provide us the emotional and practical support we needed at the time.

Fourth, God gave me the inner strength to be able to stand and not fall or go into depression or anything like that. Physically too, I was strong amid all the sleepless nights. I did not catch a cold or anything like that. I was taking medication for my blood pressure. In fact, my blood pressure read the lowest at this time because usually, one would have expected it to skyrocket, but no. God knew everything because He is the One who has the number of our days in His plan. *"Who has known the mind of the Lord? Or who has been his counsellor?"* Romans 11:34 (NIV).

There were some obstacles, as well. The first had to do with medical aid cover for the family. The usual procedure was that medical contributions were taken from salaries and the Corporation put in its contribution. Now that benefits had been paid out, ZBC wanted me to pay my own contribution six months in advance before making their contribution.

I could not afford this for my children, so I had to drop out of medical cover, and I prayed that the Lord would protect them. I was covered by my employer, EE III. During this time, three of the boys were playing rugby, and one was playing cricket and hockey. There were injuries, but no one ever needed hospitalisation. Everyone was healthy and strong, which was a gift from the Lord.

10

MY JOURNEY WITHOUT FERDINAND

When the journey began on my own, I knew I would never be able to do anything without God's help. In one of my prayer times, God led me to Psalm 91, the whole chapter;

He who dwells in the shelter of the Most High
will abide in the shadow of the Almighty.
I will say to the LORD, "My refuge and my fortress,
my God, in whom I trust."
For he will deliver you from the snare of the fowler
and from the deadly pestilence.
He will cover you with his pinions,
and under his wings you will find refuge;
his faithfulness is a shield and buckler.
You will not fear the terror of the night,
nor the arrow that flies by day,
nor the pestilence that stalks in darkness,
nor the destruction that wastes at noonday.

A thousand may fall at your side,
ten thousand at your right hand,
but it will not come near you.
You will only look with your eyes
and see the recompense of the wicked.

Because you have made the LORD your dwelling place—
the Most High, who is my refuge—
no evil shall be allowed to befall you,
no plague come near your tent.

For he will command his angels concerning you
to guard you in all your ways.
On their hands they will bear you up,
lest you strike your foot against a stone.
You will tread on the lion and the adder;
the young lion and the serpent you will trample underfoot.

"Because he holds fast to me in love, I will deliver him;
I will protect him, because he knows my name.
When he calls to me, I will answer him;
I will be with him in trouble;
I will rescue him and honor him.
With long life I will satisfy him
and show him my salvation."
Psalm 91 (ESV)

Never had a scripture been so alive and practical as this Psalm was to me then. Every verse, every line felt as if it had been written for me. I prayed verses 5 and 6 for my children, and

I asked for protection of every kind for them, including against illness. I felt helpless and vulnerable, but God picked me up through this Psalm and gave me the strength to stand up and walk. I spent hours praying before bedtime, meditating especially on verses 1, 2, and 9 to 16. This Psalm sustained and nourished me for many months, especially since I did not belong to a small group or bible study.

Sustained by Prayer and Fellowship

Over the following year, God provided people who supported me in my faith. Every Wednesday morning before work, I prayed with my wonderful friend Janet Cunningham, who has since gone to be with the Lord. She was a great comforter and a prayer warrior, and we prayed for our children, their spiritual lives, education, jobs, ministries, businesses and our grandchildren. We covered everything in those 30 minutes.

On another evening I prayed with my cousin Nomsa Moyo and once a week I would meet with my friend Jester Mlilo. On Wednesday evenings, I attended homegroup, where I met with others from church in each other's homes for bible study, prayer and fellowship. These were Jethro & Doris Dube, Catherine Mahaja, Nomsa Moyo, Jester Mlilo, Abe & Mildred Yoder, Jake & Nancy Shenk, Danisa & Trezia Ndlovu, Glen & Linda Pierce and others who served at Youngways, a nearby BICC missionary residence. They were the lifeblood that kept me strong and steady at the time when I could have easily lost my spiritual strength.

At home, we continued with our daily evening devotions, which I always led. Through these, I realised that my children loved to read the Bible. They took turns to read a few verses before passing the Bible onto the next person. To give them each

Our home group in Matshemhlophe

their own Bible, I ordered a full box of twenty. Some of them must have been given away to friends because in a short time there were no extras. We used Our Daily Bread to guide us on each day's scripture, then had a discussion, which deepened with time as the children got older.

During this period there was no money for Christmas presents for my children, but one year, I purchased the annual Daily Bread booklets and wrapped them and put one in each of their bedrooms because by then they were enjoying their individual devotions. I am very grateful for the Scripture Union Camps where they learnt how to do 'quiet time'; that is reading the Bible and praying by themselves every morning or evening, whatever time they decided on.

They also attended a camp every December before Christmas, called Youth Encounter. It was a fantastic camp for teens, run over a week, usually at Mazvikadei Dam, and helped

With (l-r) Seluleko, Samu and Selusiwe after they completed EE
at Mpopoma BICC **(1995)**

to develop their faith and equip them for a godly life as teenagers. At first, they attended as participants, but later some of them went there as leaders. I look back and see the grace of God in providing those opportunities for them. I cannot forget those men and women who gave up their time for those long days away from their families to help young people.

Education

School went well, and everyone tried their best. Whenever one of them received a good report or award from school, we celebrated with a cake and the word was, "You have done well for us all!" which was a great encouragement. Sitho went to Khumalo Primary School because when we moved from Harare, I could not get him into nearby Petra Primary. He attended CBC for High School. Selusiwe and Sibs went to Milton High and later did their 'A' Levels at CBC. Samu went to Townsend High School but could not get the right subjects there for continuity, so she went to BASS, the Seventh-Day Adventist High School. Siziwe was already at Solusi University, about an hour away from home, and CJ was working at Phillips Electrical in Harare.

All the boys made it to Zimbabwe or Matabeleland first teams in basketball, rugby, cricket and hockey. Due to the limited budget, sports socks and other training kit had to be washed daily and hung behind the freezer to dry overnight. Some people thought that the boys were spending too much time playing sport, but I found that the more they played, the better for them for two reasons. First, they had to be focused in doing their homework to have time for practice. Secondly, they were tired in the evenings so had no time for entertainment such as TV.

Worship

At first, all of us attended Brethren In Christ Church, but later on, the children chose where they wanted to fellowship. Seluleko helped with the youth at BIC Central Church for a while but later moved to the Rock Christian Church, a new church which met at the Hotel Rio, led by Rob & Gill McFarlane, and which the others were already attending. It was difficult to see them leave our family church, but I joined them for a few services at their new church to make sure that salvation through faith in Jesus Christ was the central message. Once I was satisfied that there was sound doctrine, I was happy to let them go. Sitho went to the Baptist Church where he later became the Youth Leader.

After the Sunday church services, we all came home for lunch and shared the messages we had heard from the three different churches. On Friday evenings, they frequented youth meetings at the Baptist Church. I knew that the first hour was for games and refreshments, and the second for Bible teaching, so during that time, I would pray for them and their leaders. I prayed that the Lord would open their minds and their hearts to his word, not only them but all the young people that were in the group. Every Friday, whenever I was at home, that was my occupation. I found something to do instead of being lonely and depressed.

I am very grateful to The Baptist Church for providing that opportunity and to the Youth Pastor, Ray Motsi, who later became the lead pastor. He became like an uncle to my children. I am also grateful to Rob McFarlane at the Rock Church, who cultivated a passion for Word in my children and gave them opportunities to grow in ministry, such as leading home groups. They attended Bible school through the Rock and also completed EE III training.

Indeed, the Lord was walking with us all. Ferdinand had a desire for the children to graduate from university and had always encouraged them to aim high. For his sake, I am glad that they have all since done so. Siziwe graduated from Solusi University with an Accounting Degree, and Seluleko from the University of Zimbabwe in Civil Engineering, Selusiwe from NUST in Accounting, Sibs from UZ in Engineering as a Surveyor, Samu from Solusi in Accounting but did her Articles with UNISA, Sitho in Accounting with UNISA attached to the accountant firm Deloittes. CJ later graduated at McMaster in Canada. Isn't God excellent and faithful! Isn't He a God of wonders!

Meeting my Needs According to His Riches

My husband's retirement package was significant, but due to sharply rising inflation in the country at the time, its value was greatly diminished, so it was not able to fully sustain the children's education. For example, Seluleko had secured a place at the University of Cape Town to study Architecture. However, I said to him if he went to South Africa, there would not be enough fees for his siblings. So, he chose to stay at UZ, which didn't offer his preferred Architecture and he had to study Civil Engineering. It was painful to say that to him knowing his potential, but that was beyond my circumstances then. When he started at UZ, he was awarded a bursary by Bulawayo City Council to study Civil Engineering, which meant that his fees and university expenses were covered. I thank George Mlilo, Jester's husband and City Engineer, who directed him to the opportunity. That was the faithfulness of God.

Sibs' CBC cricket team was meant to tour Durban one time, but because they had to pay their way, he was not able to go. The children missed a few chances here and there, but that is part of life. I am thankful to the Lord for what He did. I am very grateful to CBC because they allowed me to pay school fees in instalments, which made it possible for my sons to continue to attend. The God of mercy provided in His many uncommon ways. *"A father to the fatherless, a defender of widows..."* Psalm 68:5a (NIV) is what He was.

Over the years, the Lord has brought people into my life who have given me great help when I needed it most. One such family were the Cunninghams, David and Janet. I first met them in Harare, when we both attended Northside Community Church. In fact, it was through their work at Scripture Union that Northside came into being. I understand that they had gathered children at nearby Vainona Primary School for meetings, and over time these grew into Northside Community Church.

Soon after Ferdinand passed away, they happened to move to Bulawayo too. Janet looked for me, and we met occasionally for prayer, and before long, we were doing ministry together. Those who knew this dynamic lady will know what I am talking about. She invited us as a family to meet at their home on Friday evenings for games and later to share a word with the young people. Janet would not do such things without providing refreshments, which were much loved by the children.

After some time, the teenagers moved on to the Baptist youth group. Renee, David and Janet's youngest, was the same age as Sitho. So, he started to meet with them and other friends of the same age group. This went on until they also moved on to young adult groups when they were older. These youngsters developed in their spiritual walk with the Lord. David was always there with us, joined in the games with us and led lessons during his turn. The Cunninghams were a fine couple and a wonderful gift to the church as a whole.

Over the long Easter weekends, we attended family camps that they organised at Shalom Campsite. There they created many opportunities for young leaders to develop, and I saw my children take these on and grow. What amazed me about David and Janet is the way they were able to help and encourage young people in such a way that they would gain confidence and start serving in whichever position they were assigned. They helped my children to develop and reach their potential because they would entrust them with a responsibility that I sometimes thought was too big for them.

I believe that God provided David as a spiritual father to my boys because there is a time when boys need a father figure. They had someone they respected in the Lord, who was there for them in the background. Part of his legacy is that they grew into fine young men who love the Lord.

Later, some of my children were employed in their sons' businesses at one time or another. First was Siziwe, who was employed at the Hopedale farm and ostrich business after completing her degree at Solusi University. CJ ran the poultry production facility at Hamara Eggs before he left for Canada. Seluleko is the one who worked the longest with Peter Cunningham at Ostrindo, a producer of ostrich meat and leather. He developed and ran the tannery. Selusiwe and Samu also did accounts part-time there for a short period until they moved on. Sitho worked for Family Impact, a family-focused ministry led by the Cunninghams.

Once, when Samu was at Solusi University, I had an urgent need for finances. She was not able to register for her second year unless the fees had been paid upfront and in full. I had been expecting some money, but it had been delayed, and I was desperate. The Cunninghams wrote me a cheque for the amount that I needed, and when I paid them back, they gave me some of it to help with her other expenses. What can I say? All I can say is, they were brought into my life by the Omniscient God; the all-knowing God.

More Blessings - Weddings

As parents, one of the things we desire for our children once they have completed their educational pursuits and have settled into employment is for them to find their soul mates, get married and Lord willing, start their own families. Our family was blessed to experience God's love in all these areas. When my husband passed away, my youngest of seven children was eleven years old, and most were in their teens. I did not know how I would cope with raising them, seeing them through their schooling and onto happy and independent lives with families of their own. One of the reasons I so delighted in their weddings was that they were a testimony of God's faithfulness to me over the years. They were proof to me that I could say, like David in Psalm 121, *"I lift my eyes to the hills. From where does my help come? My help comes from the Lord, who made heaven and earth"* (NIV).

First to get married was CJ, our firstborn. He married Dorothy in December 1993 in Bulawayo. Two cows were prepared for them for the wedding feast. One was from Shake, Ferdinand's home village and the other from my brother Enoch in Gwatemba. My uncle Mr J D Ndlovu and his wife also provided a sheep to cater to our many guests. Countless family members gave freely of their experience and resources. Some brought firewood or vegetables, others took on roles and tasks that were important in making the wedding a success. I was overwhelmed by their often-sacrificial generosity. I praise the Lord for bringing many hearts together to stand with me.

In our culture, the wedding is hosted by the groom's family. My husband had been gone for two years. I could not have done it without the help of my father-in-law, my husband's brothers Ernest, Kenneth and Donald, together with my sister-in-law Verna and her husband Canaan. I remember one loving lady at church saying to me that it was evident that there had been a lot of prayer behind the scenes because of the success of that wedding.

Next was Siziwe who married Anthony in 1998. It caused much excitement, as she was the first daughter to be married among Ferdinand's siblings. It meant that, culturally, we received *amalobolo* from the groom and his family, which was a new experience. It was a charming wedding held at the same venue as CJ's wedding. This time we had a bit more experience holding a wedding, so were better prepared for the joyful chaos that a wedding involves. Again, I thank God for the unity of the family because, without it, it would have been impossible to get everything done. God blessed us.

Three years later, as happy as it was unexpected, there was another wedding and our fourth boy was married, before numbers two and three. Sibs had found Rumbi while they were both serving in ministry at River of Life Church in Harare. They knew in June that they wanted to get married, were engaged in September and so we only had a few months to prepare for the wedding on 15 December 2001. Again, the Lord undertook for us. The venue had become an issue because in those days people usually booked a year in advance and so there were no suitable venues by the time they started looking.

Through the Lord's kindness, we found a place on a farm in the outskirts of Bulawayo. PJ Smyth, who was their Pastor, married them in Harare. It was a beautiful ceremony. The following weekend we held the wedding reception in Bulawayo. We enjoyed the day with our guests from Rumbi's family. My friend from church, Thoko Ndlovu, did the catering and prepared a delicious meal for us.

The following year in 2002 Seluleko and Busi were married

Delegation to Gaborone for *amalobolo* meeting
for Selu & Busi's wedding (2002)

in Botswana. This wedding had challenges of its own kind. As part of building relationships between the bride and groom's families, *amalobolo* (bride price) are 'paid' to the bride's family before the wedding. The negotiations for these involved two 12-hour round trips to Gaborone for our delegation, and I was very grateful to my husband's close friend Boniface Ndimande from childhood for leading this, and to all those who travelled.

According to custom, *amalobolo* had to be paid in live cows delivered to Busi's family home in Moshupa, an hour west of Gaborone. Due to an outbreak of foot and mouth disease, we could not move any cattle from across the border in Zimbabwe as would have been the case under normal circumstances. We had to make local purchases from villages nearby, which came with its own challenges, but God undertook for us, and all went well.

The second difficulty we faced was obtaining petrol. This was a time when fuel was in extremely short supply in Zimbabwe. Some family and friends who travelled to Botswana spent the night in the fuel queue, but early in the morning, ET (private commuter buses) drivers jumped the line and pushed to the front. Our family members who had waited to get fuel the whole night got nothing. However, the Lord of mercy was looking out for us. My niece Sanelisiwe, and her husband Lovemore had 40 litres of petrol which enabled us to travel. We started off late in the morning and arrived there at 9.00 pm. Once we arrived, we were well looked after by our hosts for the week that we were there, something for which I am deeply grateful to Busi's family, the Mookas.

The first wedding reception was held at her rural home in Moshupa, incorporating much tradition and custom and with a lot of food. The second was attended by over 500 guests and held in an enormous hall in Gaborone. It was so beautiful. The third and final reception was back in Bulawayo at the Trade Fair Showgrounds. It was such a joyous occasion. We praised the Lord for all his faithfulness.

Samu and Rufaro were married next, at the Nesbitt Castle, in a beautiful garden setting in Bulawayo. Leading up to it, Rufaro faced a daunting challenge in transporting two live cows to the Shake homestead for *amalobolo*. Samu's uncles demanded this. It was tough. He talks about how exhausted he was at the end of it. Their Pastor PJ Smyth joined them in marriage in the late afternoon on a beautiful day in March. Her brother Seluleko gave away the beautiful bride. The following weekend we were all in Harare for a large wedding which was well put together by the Chitsike family. We had a great time. The evening was characterised by joyful dancing.

The following year on 2 July 2005 we had a wedding far away in England. This time it was Selusiwe and Cara who tied the knot in Bude, Cornwall, at Cara's family home. Due to the distance and cost involved no relatives from Zimbabwe were able to attend. The only family present were those that live in the UK; my sister Agneta, her husband Moffat Thebe and family, my other sister Ebbie, her husband Stephane and their son. Mr and Mrs Tobaiwa, Sibs' in-laws and my nephews Philani, Nda and his wife Nonto added to our number. I had never attended a British wedding before, found it quite different, but I thoroughly enjoyed it. The ceremony featured lots of joyous worship and Sibs preached a good sermon before Roger, Cara's dad, joined them in marriage.

Afterwards, the reception was held on a beautiful farm. I appreciate Cara's parents, Roger and Janice, for the warm welcome, for such a wonderful wedding, and am grateful to the lovely families who hosted us. Later, in 2006 we had a reception for Selusiwe and Cara in Bulawayo at The Holiday Inn. This was to welcome the bride home the Zimbabwean way. We had a great time with family and friends.

Three days later the last of our children was married when Sitho and Miranda were united on 24 June 2006 at the Bulawayo Baptist Church. Right from childhood, Sitho had been a stickler for time. His famous words to Miranda on the wedding day were, "You will be at church at 11.45am or else..." I heard that and thought to myself, or else what? We didn't get to find out because Miranda made it on time! At 11.45am on the dot, she was parked outside the church, making her one of the few brides I have seen do so. It was a "Well done Miranda" occasion. Our thanks go to Pastor Ray Motsi, who joined them and had pastored Sitho from his early days in Bulawayo.

We can never predict the events of any day that God gives us. On the morning of Sitho's wedding, as we were getting ready to leave for church, my husband's brother, Kenneth Sibanda, who had been unwell in hospital, passed away. It was a challenging day because part of the family could not attend the wedding. For those who did, how could they express joy and celebration in that kind of atmosphere? It was too late to postpone the wedding. By God's grace, we proceeded. By the end of that day, I had seven daughters and seven sons in my family.

Over the years, I have sometimes thought of how much Ferdinand would have enjoyed the weddings of his children. I remember that during the good years he was thinking ahead that we should build a cottage on the property in Matsheumhlophe so that when children got married, they would have somewhere to stay before finding their own homes. My husband had, by the time of his death, started planting an orchard, saying that when the grandchildren came to visit there would be lots of fruit for them to enjoy. He imagined that this would entice them to visit more often. I always marvelled at his vision which was prompted by the love he had for his children.

When his brother got married, Ferdinand gave all the money he could spare so that the wedding preparation should not be delayed by shortages of any necessities. From that act of willingness to share what he had, I assume he would have done the same or even more for his children. First of all, he would probably have helped them with *amalobolo*. Secondly, he would have advised and been involved in all the arrangements way ahead of time. That was how he participated in all family life. All his relatives in his ancestral home of Diana's Pool would have been notified. Different functions would have been assigned to them according to their customary family roles.

Ferdinand saw food as an essential part of fellowship and celebration and delighted in ensuring that there was always plenty. I am sure he would have slaughtered a cow or two for each of his children's wedding celebrations to make sure that everyone was well fed. On each of the wedding days, I am sure he would have been overjoyed. He would have expressed his feelings with speech and dancing. He had a very tender heart for children, and I am sure his grandchildren would have enjoyed his cuddles. In my mind's eye, I can see him surrounded by his grandchildren as he told them stories and listened with delight as they told him theirs.

11

EVANGELISM EXPLOSION MINISTRY

In 1988, while I was still in Harare, I started my training in Evangelism Explosion III (EE) through Northside Church. EE is a one-to-one evangelism tool used by churches to fulfil the mandate that Jesus issued his disciples in Matthew 28:18-19, to go and make disciples of all nations. It uses an outline to equip Christians to present the gospel using scripture and their personal testimony. Developed by the late Dr James Kennedy at his Coral Ridge Presbyterian Church in Florida in 1967, it has since spread to most countries around the world. EE works by training church leaders who in turn can equip their members for the work of personal evangelism.

My training started with a 45-min lesson at seven in the evening, after which we would go out to visit homes by appointment. Sometimes, for whatever reason, such a meeting was cancelled at short notice so the team would go knocking on doors unplanned. That sounds difficult and scary, but God always opened people's hearts, and the gospel would be presented. Teams were made up of three people, one man and two women or vice versa. The visits lasted up to an hour, and afterwards, we would return and report back to the bigger group. That was one of the exciting parts of the evening, to hear what experience each team had.

The best experience was when people who were visited responded to the gospel and received Jesus Christ as Lord and Saviour of their lives. The evening's training ended with refreshments, which meant that I arrived home at 10 pm, the latest I had ever regularly done this on my own. The road home included a long stretch that was used by large army trucks, responsible for a large number of road accidents and I have always looked back and marvelled at the faithfulness of God, just how much he protected me over that year as I drove home by myself.

Pastor Ian Wilsher led this ministry at Northside. He delivered all the lectures, but each trainee had a personal trainer who would meet with them during the week before the next lesson. My trainer's name was Helen, and she really committed herself and helped me through because EE had a long outline to be memorised. I appreciated her so much. Furthermore, every trainee had to have two prayer partners that met with him/her once a week before the lesson. This is crucial because winning souls is a spiritual battle that needs to be fought through prayer. Two weeks into the training, the Lord reminded me about the dream that I shared earlier, of the many nations singing a hymn. Therefore, I felt that the Lord's calling on my life to share His love to the lost was confirmed, and I joined as a trainer.

What I noticed was that while we were nervous before sharing the gospel, the people that we visited were also apprehensive because they did not know what to expect. I recall a young couple that we saw and who were so anxious about what was going to take place that they asked another couple to sit in with them. To our surprise, having expected to see two people, we found two couples instead. After they had heard the gospel, the Lord opened their hearts, and they all invited Jesus into their lives.

Only afterwards did they tell us that they had asked his sister and her husband to join them because church people were due to visit, and they needed support for the unexpected. This young man, the new Christian did not have time to join the visiting teams as he was running his father's business, so he offered his car with a full tank to be used for EE visits. We saw many genuine commitments and were elated whenever someone received salvation. Time and again, I saw the Lord at work as we shared the good news of Jesus Christ.

Over that year, we saw almost one hundred people go through the training. Those who were trained filled different roles in the church. Some went on to teach others and lead them on home visits. Others joined the prayer team to support those going out, and still others mentored the new believers. Often EE had a transforming effect on the lives of men and women. For example, one farmer converted his tobacco farm into a dairy one at a significant loss due to his conviction that he could not grow tobacco on the one hand and on the other tell people that it was wrong to smoke. Evangelism is the backbone of church life. I firmly believe that Jesus started the work and left it for the church to continue.

EE Assistant to Pastor

For nearly two years, I continued to train others and accompany trainees on home visits every Thursday. Then in 1989, the church asked me to join the staff full-time as the Pastor's helper, specifically to assist with the EE programme. Some of my roles included keeping records of and contacting visitors to our Sunday services, making appointments for home visits by the EE teams and making sure all who had been visited got a second visit, especially those who had committed their lives to Christ.

We found that without a proper system, some people come to church once or even twice without anyone noticing them, more so as the church grew bigger. The problem is that without contact or visitation afterwards, some of those people would not return to church after their initial visit. Outreach is not an option or extra activity for a church, but a command from our Lord and Saviour Jesus Christ. I believe every church should have an outreach team or more. Churches do not have to use the EE method but should find a way that works for them to bring the lost to the Lord.

One of the ladies that we trained, Sandy, was working at St Giles Rehabilitation Centre as an Occupational Therapist. She had a heart for her patients, and so she made appointments for the teams to visit. Most of those that we spoke to came to Christ, so once a week, I had a discipleship class with them, teaching about their new faith and showing them scriptures that would help them to grow.

I saw paraplegic men finding hope in their almost hopeless situation. It was touching to see some whose wives and families had abandoned, and no longer visited them. I remember one of them asking for a stamp to write to his children because his wife had stopped communicating with him, but he longed to see his children again. Christ gives hope when all hope is lost.

EE Work Continues in Bulawayo

After our move to Bulawayo, I was keen to use EE within whichever church we joined. However, when I contacted the EE office, whose national headquarters was in Bulawayo, they had a vacancy and so asked me to join their staff. I worked half-day, which suited me as it was during Ferdinand's illness and so I was able to look after him in the afternoons.

I joined Agrippa Dube, who ran EE, as the only other staff member, my position being Secretary/Administrator. Part of my role was to staff the office and to plan and organise training clinics. I took over from Margaret Hadebe, a very committed Christian and hard worker. She had a word for me when she was handing over her responsibilities to me. She said she felt the Lord saying I had to look after His Body, the Church, and He was going to look after mine. I believe that word was fulfilled in that while my husband's condition deteriorated, there was not a day that I had to rush home to attend to him.

Firstly, the only day I missed work was on his last day. Secondly, my children went to school like everybody else's, and the Lord provided in every way. Not only them, but God did look after my body in a remarkable way, which He still does. It was a blessing to work at the EE office because we started each day with a scripture reading and prayer, which was of vital spiritual support for me, especially after Ferdinand died. The work of evangelism itself was an act of supernatural conflict which kept us on our knees and taught us to depend on Jesus, who said,

"...for apart from me you can do nothing" John 15:5b (ESV).

EE, as a non-profit organisation had limited funds that were donated by well-wishers, so the salaries were very minimal. In my case, it was not about money but the fulfilment of serving the Lord. After Ferdinand died, someone offered me a job in teaching, to help with my income, but I felt that God had called me to work at EE. I believed that the Lord would take care of my needs, and to this day, He has never let me down

Expansion of EE Work in Bulawayo

As the work at the EE office expanded, it became necessary to take on another helper. Gloria Ndlovu, a very humble and capable lady, was employed as a secretary and administrator. That allowed me to help Agrippa Dube in fieldwork which involved promoting the EE ministry in new areas and churches. I now had the opportunity to introduce EE to BIC churches as well, because until then, it had not been running in any of our congregations. It was not easy to convince BIC pastors that EE was an effective means of sharing the gospel. But God being God, in His mysterious ways He enabled a breakthrough. I had a meeting with the Bishop, Martin Senda, who was receptive to my proposal to use EE as part of outreach evangelism and arranged training for all the Bulawayo-area Pastors.

One of my fieldwork activities was organising training clinics and semesters for Pastors, leaders and lay-people from different churches. A clinic is where Pastors and leaders come together for a week to cover the twelve lessons of the course, including home visits. In a semester, the same classes are spread out, with one per evening over twelve weeks. This works better in urban churches since participants can attend after work.

As the work spread into rural areas, we had to do things differently. We ran a week of everyday lessons, then planned another one later to complete them. Seeing God work through EE among both the learned and the illiterate in the church was an incredible privilege. In Romans 1:14 Paul says; *"I am a debtor both to Greeks and non-Greeks, both to the wise and the foolish" (NIV)*. My background as a teacher was useful in helping other trainers understand the difference between teaching and preaching. I found that trainees learnt the EE outline better through training and example than through a sermon-style presentation, something that was easy for some trainers to slip into. The lessons were later translated into Ndebele, Shona and Tonga, which made EE more accessible to many more people in rural and urban areas.

Where there were people who could not read in any language, we used different tools to aid the training. For example, there was an occasion in a remote area of Tonga-speaking Binga, where we once used the Jesus film to help people who could not read or write. An elderly woman was deeply moved after the screening, saying, "I may not be able to read the Bible, but today I saw it with my own eyes." It was touching to see her joy in seeing Jesus' gift on the cross revealed as never before.

Some of the rural areas were remote, difficult to access, and the transport unreliable. This was especially true of *emaguswini*; the forests of Matabeleland that lie between Bulawayo and Victoria Falls. Sometimes, however, this would present opportunities, such as on one trip to Mzola 27, which was five hours by bus from Bulawayo. We had hardly travelled 60 km from the city when the bus broke down in a bushy area. There seemed to be no hope that we would get moving anytime soon since we were far from anywhere that the bus operators could get help. I thought of looking for a lift back to the city, without considering that the breakdown might be part of God's plan.

An Opportunity to Share the Gospel

It was around ten o'clock in the morning, under a pleasantly warm winter sun in June, so most of us got off the bus and sat on the grass. Suddenly, the thought came to me that I could take that time to share the gospel with some people instead of just sitting. So, I called two ladies together, and I shared the gospel with them. They prayed to receive Christ as Lord and Saviour of their lives, right there. A few minutes after we finished, the bus operators who had been working on the bus told us to prepare to leave. One of those ladies remarked that the reason the bus had broken down was for them to hear the gospel. It was thrilling to see how the Lord works without our human planning.

In the BICC, Overseers are leaders who work under the Bishop to manage all the churches in a district. I worked with them to organise training in their regions. The first Overseer that I worked with was Rev Cornelius Ngwenya, a humble man who did his best under exceedingly challenging circumstances. He had no transport, which was difficult as his District, Nono, included some of the most isolated and difficult-to-access churches of any. Also, since his salary came from churches in his District, and almost all of these were in remote areas where people had no access to markets, he had practically no income.

I remember the first time he and I went from Bulawayo to Gegema to teach Sunday School lessons. We arrived at the bus terminus in the morning for a bus to wait for a bus that only appeared 7 hrs later, then travelled on it for another 6 hrs before reaching our destination late at night. I was surprised to see how difficult it was to walk in the deep sandy soil of *emaguswini*. This was the first of many because I was on the BICC Christian Education Committee for several years, and we had decided to each concentrate on a district, Nono being mine.

I worked with Rev Emmanuel Chidziva, who had been my Pastor many years before in Glen Norah and now an Overseer, in Tsholotsho and we conducted training at Pumula Mission for the first time. Then I worked with Jabulani Mudenda in Lupane, training church leaders at Mzola 5, Mzola 27 and Binga. He later joined the full-time staff at EE as a fieldworker. Later, Rev Teddious Moyo took over from Jabulani as the Overseer, and we covered more churches, training leaders in EE.

Three well-trained men in Binga served the church there exceedingly well; Thomas Dube, Stephen Chuma and Muzamba. I worked with them a lot in Binga and Lupane. At some stage, EE received a donation of bicycles from the US through Harold Peasley at EE Pretoria, and this was of immense help to them in reaching more churches for evangelism work. Over the years, I have seen donations and support from churches within and outside Zimbabwe significantly advance the work of the gospel.

One time I had a class to run at Tinde in Binga, along with Stephen and Muzamba. I travelled by bus from Bulawayo, and we had arranged that they were going to meet me in a donkey cart at my stop. When I disembarked at 6:00 pm, there they were on bicycles. They had been unable to find donkeys to use because they were unfamiliar with people in the area. I had a choice to make; to stay there for the night, at this bus stop was just an unmarked spot beside the road deep in the forest, and board the bus back into town the following day, or walk nine km at night to the training venue. I thought that having travelled the whole day to get there, I should just press on. Besides, people were waiting to be trained. I decided to walk.

Thankfully, I was wearing athletic shoes for what turned out to be a 2hr walk at night. Praise the Lord, the moon provided light because this trail had rocky sections which would have been difficult to walk otherwise. At one point, I stumbled and fell, the poor guys had to help me up, and we continued walking. Finally, I saw a glimpse of light, a fire to show that we were approaching a village, the first sign of people we had seen. It was an incredible experience because when I got there, even though I was over 60 years old, I still felt strong and could have gone further. I praised the Lord because I had exceeded my usual endurance. God had renewed my body and given me new energy.

We were hosted by the woman who was the lay preacher, *umphathi*, of the church we were training. She was a wonderful lady, but her husband was not saved. So, after two days, he was not happy that we were keeping his wife from harvesting the crops. We realised that and decided that on one of the days we would wake up very early in the morning. We went to work in the fields until noon and harvested their whole crop of sorghum.

Her husband had gone away for the morning and returned home to find that not only had we completed the harvest, but we had carried the grain home. He was stunned and humbled. God has a purpose for everything because, on our next visit, we showed the Jesus film, and after watching it, he was the first one on the first night to respond to the call to salvation. He prayed the prayer of repentance and accepted Jesus. We had to do the same in many places because we did not want to offend the husbands if the wives were in training, and noted how these acts of humility were able to soften people's hearts towards the gospel.

A Victory for the Gospel

In Jambesi an hour east of the Victoria Falls, in an area called Ndlovu, we met a lady called MaNcube. When we visited her home and shared the gospel with her, she told us that she had always wanted to go to church, but no one had ever invited her. After hearing the gospel, she wanted to accept Christ, but because she was the keeper of all the family ancestral worship material, she needed to discuss this with her family. As we were talking to her, her eldest son arrived from his own homestead. Without wasting any time, she said, "My son, these people from the church say I must receive the Almighty God."

He replied, "Mama, you can receive the Almighty." It was such a beautiful moment. She prayed to receive Christ. In that area, we found many people who were open to the gospel, but they were very much caught up in ancestral worship.

I remember one man, Mr Thebe, whose wife was the preacher, *umphathi,* at the local church. After Agrippa shared the gospel with him, he repeatedly said, "If I want to receive Christ, I must first empty my hands, because I cannot receive Him if I am still holding onto my ancestral worship. My hands are full." By the time we left his village, he still had not freed his hands. I hoped and prayed that the Lord had mercy on him.

On the same trip, we came across one of Mr Thebe's neighbours whose wife was a Christian, but he was not, and we were warned that he was particularly resistant to the gospel. However, he sat in attentively on a visit we made to their house and presented the gospel. So gripped was he by the gospel that he sat by while his herd of cattle passed by heading towards his crops, which for a subsistence farmer, would have a catastrophic outcome! His wife had to run out to head them away from the fields. He decided not to receive salvation and said that he needed to think it through, but his heart was much softened towards the gospel.

In the coal-mining town, Hwange, we worked with both BICC and Methodist Churches. The Methodist Church had two women who were trained in EE and who worked hard to equip their members as well as other churches. They were Miriam Nkomo and Esther Makova, whose daughter Elizabeth had been in that car accident with my children many years previously in Harare. They coordinated the work of EE among different churches, and beyond, once bringing together local churches in the town for a revival crusade. Through their endeavours, EE flourished in Hwange and the surrounding areas as they helped to teach rural churches.

Sometime later, Miriam was elected Bishop over the whole of the Methodist Circuit in Matabeleland. That is how mature and grounded she was in the Lord.At Victoria Falls, on the northern border with Zambia, we worked with different churches as well as BICC. We spent much of our time with Pastor Ndlovu of the Pentecostal Assemblies who had a big church in the township. Many people came to Christ through the home visits that we made there.

One of the places that Jabulani Mudenda, Brighton Nkokha and myself went to was to Sanyathi, a Baptist Mission, 6 hours northeast of Bulawayo, where Pastor Dlula was serving. We trained an exceptionally committed group of people there. One of the trainees, a Mr Moyo, testified of his amazement at how much time he had wasted over the years watching TV after work instead of visiting and sharing the gospel with people. He said EE had been such an eye-opener and had caused him to re-order his life's priorities.

Taking a Step of Faith

In Wanezi BIC District we worked with Rev Elliot Msipha. I travelled with Benson Nyathi, who had joined EE staff full-time, and Mrs Violet Mlotshwa, who came from the area, in nearby Dekezi. We ran classes in the afternoon, and in the evening, Rev Msipha held a revival service mainly for young people. Nearby there was a traditional healer, *inyanga*, who had a fearsome reputation, such that the local trainees were afraid to go on home visits to his homestead. I felt nervous too, but I decided that his need for Christ was bigger than my fear, so I took a small team with me and went.

He received us well and said that he no longer believed in ancestral worship and showed us where he had burnt his charms. He had received the gospel but needed assurance, so we presented it to him. I believe that fear often needlessly hinders us from sharing the gospel, which is why prayer is such an essential partner to evangelism. We returned sometime later to run Kids EE and presented the gospel to Grade 7 pupils at the school. There was an overwhelmingly positive response to the gospel. World Vision, working hand-in-hand with us, had sponsored this training. They had done a survey and found out that most children between the age of eight and fifteen had been involved in sexual activity, so they decided that over and above the food distribution they would sponsor the sharing of the gospel. This was a very fruitful training because after that we received a letter from one of the trainees, MaNgwenya from Sidzibe saying she had presented the gospel to one of the classes in the school.

In Beitbridge, along the southern border of the country, we worked with the Baptist Church, led by Pastor Mukandatsama. The training went very well, but they did not continue for long after we left because of unrelated problems that the church had. In Gwanda we worked with a BIC church with Rev Norman Dewa. He had a good class with a lot of potential. One of the trainees was Mrs J Ncube, who was already a church planter and serving the church in the tin-mining town of Kamativi.

When we returned some time later, more churches had been coordinated, and we had a large class of Pastors and leaders. We were meant to visit for the third time to run a refresher course but could not because Pastors were pre-occupied with alleviating the effects of "Operation Murambatsvina", a government operation in 2005 to forcibly clear informal settlements, that left hundreds and thousands of people homeless.

In Gweru, our third-largest city, we trained a BICC class for a week, but it was not easy because we only met in the evening with people who had come from work. During the day we had a class of ladies who could not attend for the whole day, because of domestic duties, such as picking up their children from school. So, the training was not very fruitful.

Wonderful Support in Bulawayo

Bulawayo had many committed churches whose members continued to train year after year. The Methodist Church was the first to catch onto EE, and later almost all their congregations in the city were EE-trained. They provided the support needed to start EE in Zimbabwe, and our Board consisted mainly of people from the Methodist and Baptist churches, such as Phil Whitehead, Yvonne Walker, Thoko Makuyane and Melika Mazabane. They also provided an office for us to rent at their centrally located Main Street church, which made access easier for visitors from rural churches.

Later, the Baptist Church in the city centre became like a home for EE, because we ran most of our clinics there. The whole church supported us by making meals and serving as prayer partners under their Senior Pastor Brian Anderson, who was the chairman of the EE board for many years. After Brian left for South Africa, Alan Bradnick took his place on the Board and hugely supported our ministry financially and through his time. Both the Methodist and the Baptist churches had EE-trained members who supported us financially for many years. Only the Lord knows how many people came into His kingdom because of their sacrificial giving.

In Bubi district at Siganda, we did a lot of training under the sponsorship of World Vision. They were running projects there, as I said before they wanted to develop the whole person by sharing the gospel. Our first trip lasted a week, which we spent with a good crowd of engaged men and women. We returned sometime later to run a refresher course to support their continued work in churches.

On this second trip, I became very unwell. First, my blood pressure shot up, but there were no doctors in attendance at the local clinic. The nurses were able to help me by giving me medication. The following day, I had an infection and could keep neither food nor water down. The class was very concerned. I was almost ready to return to Bulawayo, but the class prayed for me and guess what, the Lord touched me instantly. They could not believe it when I stood up to teach. I remember one old man, Mr Dlodlo talking to others saying, "Man, have you ever seen anything like this?" The sudden infusion of energy that I felt had surprised me too. Matthew 28:19 says, *"... And lo, I am with you always, even to the end of the age"* (KJV).

In the Shadow of Great Pain

I once travelled to Mgodimasili in Tsholotsho, 3 hours northwest of Bulawayo, for training with Benson Nyathi and Saziso Mathe, one of our trainees from Agape Mission in Bulawayo. This area suffered some of the worst atrocities of Gukurahundi, when almost all men were either massacred by the Fifth Brigade or fled to South Africa. Since then, the culture in the area is that all the young men and many schoolboys leave to find work in South Africa and so there are only women and older men who have retired. Therefore, the class was attended by older women who were looking after their grandchildren, whose parents worked in South Africa, and so the training was not very successful.

We heard many harrowing stories of torture, anguish and loss during the Gukurahundi. Such is the trauma that the culture is different from other places in Matabeleland, for example, for home visits, we had to announce our presence from a distance. We could not approach the home directly as we could elsewhere. Those we trained gained much from the course, but we found the community a tough place for the gospel to take root, and yet the message of the cross of healing and reconciliation was most necessary there. The chief was said to lament the loss of the BIC church, closed during Gukurahundi, saying that its presence had been beneficial for the community.

A wonderful lady who loved the Lord hosted and took good care of us. I fell ill again, this time with a raging fever and completely drained of strength. We planned to leave on the following morning but I was too weak to drive and as the only driver on the team we couldn't leave. We prayed, our loving Lord healed me, and I was able to complete the whole week as planned. Praise the Lord!

Reflections on Evangelism as Ministry

Although I found the work taxing, especially in the rural areas, and with meagre resources, it was exciting and fulfilling. Little did I know when I walked into the EE offices at George Silundika Aveue on my first day that this was the ministry that would occupy the last part of my working life. Following 17 years of working for EE, here are some of my reflections on evangelism as a ministry.

1. *Evangelism changes the priorities of a church.* I found that when a Pastor and in turn, the congregation, caught a vision for evangelism, it changed their perspectives about their purpose. Home visits make them have a greater desire to see their local communities reached for Christ, and they change what they do, to make this happen. An example was the BIC church in Nkulumane, a township on the eastern boundary of Bulawayo. Benson Nyathi had done EE and struggled to convince his church leaders to adopt it until he took some of them one-by-one on home visits in the area. They were so moved by how effective this personal evangelism was that they adopted EE and within a

year had welcomed 50 new converts from the surrounding homes. Not only that but they re-arranged their budget priorities to fund local outreach and materials for trainees. They are still running EE to this day.

2. *The gospel transforms lives.* Some of the most passionate Christians I have met are those whose hearts burn with a desire to see the lost saved. Over the years, I have seen people saved through EE home visits whose lives were utterly transformed. People such as lawyer Dudley Pate who left a successful legal practice to learn Portuguese and minister in Mozambique.

3. *Evangelism unites Christians.* In our training, we had Pastors and Church leaders from mainline as well as Pentecostal Churches; those that fall under Zimbabwe Council of Churches and those that come under Evangelical Fellowship of Zimbabwe. Some of our training was attended by leaders and lay-people from different churches, and we saw the shared purpose of the Great Commission unite Christians, resulting in many joint efforts in local ministry. This did not apply just between churches, but members of the same congregation often found their bonds deepened as they prayed for one another and witnessed side-by-side to win souls for Christ.

4. *Prayer is essential for evangelism.* In EE training, every trainee had to have two prayer partners because winning souls is mainly a spiritual battle, that individuals by themselves cannot win. The devil fights on all fronts, and the outcome of any training we ran very much relied on support from intercessors. I lost count of how often trainers or trainees would face sudden obstacles just before or be called for sickness, death or other family urgencies during the course. It did not take long for most churches that did EE to develop prayer groups as they realised

how Satan attacks every effort to share the gospel.

5. *Evangelism benefits from partnerships.* Whenever we could, we partnered with organisations when it allowed us greater access to areas and people. For example, the World Vision distributes food aid, but their main aim is to contribute to the development of the whole person, including spiritually. Therefore, in all the places where they had projects, they sponsored EE to train the rural people that they were helping. Such as at Jahe, ten kilometres before Tsholotsho Centre. We ran a course there, and when the teams went out to share the gospel, Chief Mathema received Christ as his Lord and Savior.

We also worked with a charity called Family Impact, which promoted healthy families. They sponsored EE training for the rural people they were supporting in an ostrich project in Mbembesi, Kezi and Mawabeni. An ostrich farming business, run by Peter Cunningham, worked with the farmers, providing them ostrich chicks to grow and sell back to them. Such partnerships made it possible to supply training materials which the rural people could not otherwise afford.

A God of Miracles

Over the years, I have seen God move miraculously to allow people the opportunity to accept salvation. Here are a few of them

The Lord isn't really being slow about his promise, as some people think. No, he is being patient for your sake. He does not want anyone to be destroyed but wants everyone to repent (2 Peter 3:9, NLT).

Mbembesi

In Mbembesi, an hour east of Bulawayo, my team visited a home where a ninety-year-old woman lived, Gogo MaNtolo. When we started sharing the gospel with her family, they told us not to worry about her because she was deaf. Afterwards, when some members of the household prayed to receive Christ, Gogo MaNtolo also prayed with them! A miracle had happened, and her hearing had been restored! Everyone was amazed that she had heard the gospel and responded to the call to salvation.

Mzola 55, Lupane

We had a week's training session at Mzola 55 in Lupane starting on a Monday morning. On the Thursday of that week, we led the trainees out on home visits to share the gospel. My team visited a home where a young man was critically ill and had been in that condition for the past two weeks. He was weak and bed-ridden, and his family had expected him to pass away on each of the previous days. I shared the gospel with him as briefly as I could. After I finished, he prayed to receive Christ! He was so weak that I had to put my ear to his mouth to be able to hear him pray. The following morning at 8 am, he passed away. We believed that God had kept him alive long enough to know the gospel.

Crossroads, Plumtree

Crossroads in Crossroads, Plumtree is a semi-arid area 20 km east of the Botswana border. Benson Nyathi and I went to train one of the cult churches whose Pastor had shown great interest in EE. When we started teaching, we were amazed at their eagerness to learn. We also realised that they were hearing the truths of the gospel for the first time. When we took the teams out on the third day for home visits, the Pastor's wife was in my team.

After sharing the gospel with the family, a man and his two wives prayed to receive Christ. On our way back, the Pastor's wife told me that while the man and his wives prayed, she had joined them in receiving Christ. When we arrived home, she took her husband into their bedroom and told him what she had done. She urged him to allow the whole class an opportunity to receive Christ as Lord and Saviour. "We have not done this before. We need to receive Christ," she said. So, the following morning he discussed this with us and said that we should allow his church members the opportunity to do so.

When Benson presented the gospel, the whole class of twenty men and women prayed to receive Christ! The Pastor later explained the gospel to the rest of the church, half of whom rejected this new teaching. This caused the group to split, with half of them joining the Pastor to form a new congregation under the Baptist Church. God lovingly convicted them of their error. What a marvellous God we serve.

The Challenges That We Faced

Outreach ministry was full of joys, but we also faced significant challenges, such as the following;

1.   The EE outline has to be memorised to be presented confidently. Not everyone was able to do this, not just in the rural areas, but even in the urban churches. However, later we were able to use a picture book which helped considerably.

2.   In urban churches, it is not easy to get people to commit

themselves to 12 weeks of training after work. Those who completed the entire course were excited, but once they were done, it was even more difficult for them to continue as trainers mainly because of transport costs, walking home alone safely and other pressures that people faced as the economy worsened. Nevertheless, some were able to keep going, and we saw many become pillars in their congregations, such as Saziso Mathe, who I travelled with to Mgodimasili and is still involved with EE in his local church, over 15 years later.

3.   Most of the EE's training costs were covered by donors, but we charged a nominal fee for registration and for training materials. People found it hard to pay this, especially in rural areas where their churches were unable to help them with the cost.

4.   In rural areas, training can only be done for 6 months of the year, when people are not busy in the fields. That leaves EE teams with only May to October to cover large areas of the countryside before the rains come. Planting of crops starts, and some roads become inaccessible.

5.   Also, in the rural areas, most congregations are made up almost entirely of women, and so they often do the preaching. The challenge we came across was that when a man came to Christ, it was difficult for him to sit under a woman preacher, in particular, if she was his wife. After the EE teams had gone, the men usually stopped attending church.

6.   Discipleship is generally lacking in almost every congregation, both rural and urban. This is due both to a lack of teaching materials and poor awareness of its importance among church leaders. Churches are provided material on discipleship when they do EE, which has been translated into the vernacular,

but this is often unused. I believe that we all need encouragement in the whole area of discipleship.

Reflections on Evangelism

1. First and foremost, I learnt that God loves people, and His will is that all should come to repentance (2 Peter 3:9; Ezekiel 18:31-32). In these verses, we see the heart of God. Over the years, we often saw God intervene in people's lives, guiding us to unplanned or unexpected encounters with them, which we called 'divine appointments'. I believe that salvation is the greatest of miracles, and we often felt his presence as we shared the gospel. Sometimes, in our minds, we would write off certain people because of their reputation or reaction and have met some who have written themselves off from the possibility of God loving them. However, we saw God saving all kinds of people, and learnt to believe that all can be saved.

2. Second, I learnt that people do not always reject the gospel when they hear it correctly explained. In most cases, we just invite them to church, and they wonder in their minds, "Come to Church to do what?" Yet if we would obey the Great Commission and "Go!", meeting people in their homes and telling them about how God loves them, many more will be saved (Matthew 28:19-20).

3. Third, in the Great Commission, Jesus promises to be with us till the end of the age. I have found this to be true over my years of ministry. On our trips to the rural areas, most of the buses we travelled in atrocious condition, yet we never spent a day or a night in the bush after a breakdown or accident. Once, on a trip back from Dekezi, we caught a bus that had a broken axle or some other metal rod, which the operator had replaced

with a small tree trunk. This too broke regularly, and the conductor would run into the woods with his axe to replace it, shouting *"Iqamuk' iqolo!"* (the bus's back is broken!)

4.   Fourth, we saw God provide for the work of evangelism. Over the years, the ministry often ran out of money, but the bills were always paid, we never went without pay or ever had to cancel any trips or clinics.

I praise the Lord for all the leaders He brought alongside me to equip me for this vital work, especially Agrippa Dube who has since gone to be with the Lord. He was committed to the task of evangelism and a passionate advocate of EE, leaving no stone unturned for the sake of the gospel. He was a compelling and dynamic speaker who inspired many to be involved in outreach and to contribute to EE. Working with Harold Peasley, he raised much of the funding we needed from abroad. I learnt a lot from and worked well with him. I thank God for the opportunity to train many young men and women who now serve as leaders or pastors in their churches.

I had always known that God had called me to serve Him, but I did not know in what way. Even though I had been involved in Sunday school and other church roles for years, I felt a strong desire to share the gospel beyond that. His opening the door for me to serve in EE allowed me to live out His purposes for me, and I praise Him for seventeen fulfilling years of ministry.

12

MY INVOLVEMENT WITH BICC

I have taught Sunday School in all the Brethren-In-Christ churches that I attended - Mpopoma, Glen Norah, Bulawayo Central and Community Church. In our congregations, Sunday School is a form of interactive adult bible study that takes place an hour before the main service on Sunday mornings.

Following my return from the Haggai Institute for Leadership Training, Doris Dube, who had attended the Institute before me, and I spent several months visiting different BIC congregations to train Sunday School teachers. We found that whether teaching from a passion for it or from being asked to, all required equipping with skills and know-how to be able to serve effectively. We discussed the value of Sunday School, the preparation and presentation of lessons and the use of teaching aids for both adult and children's classes.

Teaching Sunday School at Mtshabezi

Serving on the Christian Education Committee

My passion for practical Bible teaching later led me to accept election to the Christian Education Committee, which ex-

ists to equip Sunday school teachers and develop lessons for BIC churches throughout Zimbabwe. While I was the chairperson, we organised training for teachers in each District. Churches found it difficult to pay for their teachers to attend, so in most cases, there weren't as many people as we would have liked.

Thanks to funding from George Bundy, former schools' manager at Wanezi but since retired to America, we ran a national workshop at Mpopoma. We put together Sunday school lessons from First and Second Thessalonians and asked Rev J D Ndlovu to introduce them to the teachers and Superintendents, those overseeing Sunday School in their local church. It was well-attended, and we were delighted at the large number who attended from rural churches, where the need is greatest. The whole day was a success, and I realised that my part in it had been to be faithful to God, and he had done the rest. My job was made lighter by the hard work of the committee, which included Themba Mkubo, Robert Ndlovu, Violet Mlotshwa and Ozilina Mpofu.

Serving on the BICC National Prayer Committee

The Brethren in Christ Church holds an annual meeting, The Zimbabwe Conference, for its members. This is the same kind of conference as that which took place in 1896 in Pennsylvania where the BIC decided to send missionaries to Zimbabwe. These meetings are usually held at the church's mission stations on a rotational basis, to allow every District the joy of hosting brethren from around the country. Apart from devotional and worship services, the church meets to review the year, make business decisions and elect new officers to various committees.

For many years I led the Prayer Committee which prayed for the Zimbabwe Conference, both in the lead up to it and while it was in session. We felt the enormity of this task because the smooth running, safe travel and the Christ-centredness of the conference was a spiritual battle. Because our members came from churches across the country, meeting together was often a challenge but always fruitful.

Some reading this book might wonder what we would be praying for. First and foremost, we prayed for our leaders. That would include the Bishop, the Executive Board, the Overseers and the different levels of church leadership, various committees as they put together their conference reports, the conference speakers and the hosting District. It is a massive undertaking for a District to put everything in place on time, considering there are so many congregations in every District. We would pray for these different church communities to be able to pay their dues on time so that the hosting District would not be prevented from working through a lack of funds. During the conference, we prayed for the speakers, the business sessions, as well as the catering.

We also prayed for people to be saved, revived and encouraged. The effect of prayer is not always visible to us, but we prayed fully believing that God had heard us and would answer. The conference had a prayer room where people could come for prayer, or for someone to pray with or for them. We tried to encourage people to pray for themselves even when they returned to their churches because they often lacked confidence that God would answer them as they did not consider themselves to be prayer warriors. I believe that there is no such thing as a prayer warrior but that the Lord answers every heart that cries to Him.

Serving on the MWC Prayer Committee

In 2003 I was involved in the prayer committee for the Mennonite World Conference (MWC) at a time when the need for God's intervention was especially significant. MWC is a global community of churches of which BICC is a part and holds an Assembly every 6 years. It was to be held in Africa for the first time in its history, hosted by the Brethren in Christ Church in Bulawayo. At the time, Zimbabwe was going through a severe economic crisis which made it almost impossible to host 7000 people from 65 different countries. There was a shortage of food, fuel and other supplies needed for hotels and guesthouses to accommodate that many guests. The organising committee considered relocating the conference to South Africa, but we prayed, as we had been doing for the past year and a half, that the Lord would provide all that was needed for it to continue in Zimbabwe.

Around that time one of our committee members received a scripture from the Lord, *"Every valley shall be lifted up, and every mountain and hill be made low; the uneven ground shall become level, and the rough places a plain"Isaiah 40:4 (ESV)*. This seemed to us to be confirmation that God had answered our prayer, and we were greatly encouraged. Soon after that, the organising committee decided to go ahead with holding the conference in Bulawayo.

Two weeks before the conference, we invited more people to come to the venue, which was the Trade Fair grounds for prayer and fasting. There was power in that prayer meeting. We felt it, mostly when we walked around and touched every building there. It was not the same, and everyone experienced something beyond us. On the morning before the evening start of the conference, the whole committee met to pray and fast until noon. When we left the prayer room, the entire conference venue was full of people.

Throughout the conference, we maintained a prayer room where people could come to pray or be prayed for. In the end, we had a magnificent gathering in our City of Bulawayo, and we praised God for His presence throughout the conference. What a mighty God we serve! It was not only about the prayer committee but the Lord in answering everybody who prayed and giving strength to all who worked hard in their respective assignments. It was a team effort for His honour and glory.

Serving on the Home and Family Life Committee

I once served in the Home and Family Committee for the Urban District, which prepares and facilitates teaching during the annual home and family month that BIC churches run. One of the important things we did was arrange a marriage enrichment seminar for BIC Pastors and their wives at Shalom Campsite, in the Matobo Hills. It was facilitated by David and Janet Cunningham of Family Impact.

We felt the need to give our pastors a relaxed time with their spouses which they would not usually have due to their heavy schedules. We also hoped this would serve to strengthen their relationships as spouses so that the devil does not take advantage of their busy schedules to compromise their witness. Pastors and their wives are critical to the growth of the church. I believe the seminar was fruitful, but only they can give a testimony of just how much. What I noticed as I worked with Pastors is that as a church, we overlook their social and family needs by not providing more opportunities for them and their spouses. We were grateful to all the congregations that paid for their pastors.

I was asked to contribute to a book that could be used for Home and Family. I wrote on 'How to Bring up Godly Children Including Orphans'. I am sure it was due to a lack of funding that the Literature Committee could not finish the production of this material for use in the church.

Serving in a Local Congregation

I have served in many committee roles in all the congregations I have attended. At Bulawayo Central BIC where I attended church for fourteen years, I taught adult Sunday School, served in the Main Church Committee and as a Deaconess. The position I enjoyed most was being a Deaconess because I love visiting people and connecting with new visitors to the church, some of whom became long-lasting friends.

During that time, we ran an Evangelism Explosion Class that trained, visited and made a significant impact in the church. There are people there who were trained at that time who still use EE as a way of life. Still at Bulawayo Central, I tried to start the Alpha course, which was developed in the UK but used by churches around the world to introduce non-Christians to the Christian faith. It is a course with twelve topics done once a week that include, 'Who Jesus Is', 'His Work', and these are discussed after a video presentation. This approach did not work at Central. I am not sure why it failed to take off except maybe that some programmes work better with a specific people group. In November 2003 I left to join BIC Community Church.

My Involvement at BIC Community Church

When I joined Community BIC Church, we were meeting in the Chapel at Main Street Methodist Church. Unusually for a BIC congregation in Bulawayo, preaching was in English as there were non-Ndebele speakers who attended, such as international students and faculty from the Theological College of Zimbabwe (TCZ).

It was a much smaller church than Central, but I quickly got used to it and came to love it. At the beginning of the year, at a planning meeting, Mr M T Ncube who was the chairperson of the church committee asked to step down after serving for a long time. I was immediately asked to take over and I accepted, but only reluctantly as I felt still too new to the church to lead. Our two TCZ students from Zambia had graduated and left at the end of the year, a loss we felt deeply since one of them, Harold, had been teaching Sunday School. We held the committee meetings every month where our Pastor, Lameck Nyoni gave his report, and the treasurer, Glen presented the financial statement.

In June 2004, I visited my children in Canada for six months, and in my absence, Phyllis Engle stepped in. Shortly after that, we received a generous notice period from the Methodist Church who needed the use of the building. We decided to look for a new home outside the city centre for two reasons; cost considerations, and more importantly, to find a community that did not have a church presence.

Eventually, God opened an undeveloped stand adjacent to TCZ on Gwanda Road, opposite the National University of Science and Technology (NUST) University. We thank God for the late Mr Ivin Ncube, who helped in the process of buying the property, and for the TCZ which allowed us to rent a meeting room for our services until we built our own building.

In addition to Sunday School, I had the privilege of teaching a baptism class. We had a pool of Sunday School teachers who are called on to help all the time. What a blessing this was. Whenever I have been asked to preach, I have done so with pleasure because it is not about me, but it is about Jesus. I have a deep sense of my limitations when I preach, so I pray to Jesus because He is Head of His church, He knows what His sheep need. The church committee organised a family seminar, which we asked David Cunningham to host. He did an excellent job as always. First, he talked about teenagers because most parents experience a crisis when their children get to that critical age. In the afternoon session he spoke about how couples relate to one another. It was a wonderful day.

There was a group of ladies who met for Bible study every Tuesday morning at each other's homes. I led it first, then as time went on the ladies took turns to lead. We covered many topics, which we really enjoyed, after which we enjoyed fellowship over refreshments. After a year, we decided to do Evangelism Explosion over two years, as there was not enough time to commit to it weekly.

When we started, I was still travelling to South Africa for medical treatment. When my therapy required an extended stay, I asked Benson Nyathi to take over the class. We visited many people in our area, including members of our own

Teaching Sunday School at Matopo Mission

families to share the gospel. The Lord was faithful to us. There are now fellow saints attending church with us who came to Christ through those encounters. For home visits, we sought help from trained teachers like Mrs Violet Mlotshwa and Mrs Chirawu. I enjoyed working with these ladies because of their commitment. It has been five years now, and they are still going out visiting people. They have kept going, even through some of the nation's worst political and economic problems. (Matthew 28:19-20).

On 21 August 2010, we had a memorable wedding that was hosted by the church at my home. Our Pastor Moses Kalafula, who had started attending the church as a TCZ student from the D.R. Congo, married his beautiful bride Melphine Ncube. The Marriage Officer was Rev I D Ndlovu of the UCCSA, and Rev Milson Ndlovu of Lobengula BICC preached the Word. There were

very limited resources available to conduct the wedding and reception, but the church joyfully contributed food, their labours
and whatever else was needed to make things happen.

13

Diagnosed With Cancer

In 2007, fourteen months after the wedding of my last-born son, Sitho, I was diagnosed with cancer. In August every year, I usually attend the BIC Zimbabwe Conference, which in that year was at Matopo Mission. A few days before it was due to start, I noticed an unusual feeling in my stomach whenever I had something to eat. I felt full after only a few mouthfuls. I visited my doctor, and on examination, he felt something in my stomach and sent me for a scan. The following day, I planned to do my laundry, check the results of my scan, return home, iron and pack my clothes for the Conference. The Bible says we should say; *"If it the Lord's will, we will live and do this or that"* James 4:15 (NIV).

My results contained a terrible surprise for me - the scan revealed a growth in my stomach. My doctor promptly referred me to a specialist surgeon for what he suspected was a liver tumour. All my plans for the conference were shattered. I was faced with a new challenge. I went to see the specialist surgeon that very day. He booked me in for a CT scan to more clearly identify the problem. It all happened very quickly. The following day, I had the scan done at Galen House and collected my results the next morning, which I took to the surgeon. He confirmed a tumour on the liver that needed surgery, which he said he was unable to carry out due to the unavailability of medicine in the country. He advised that I travel to England or South Africa, for which he estimated the cost to be R60,000 (USD$8,400) in South Africa. I had been accompanied there by my friend Jester Mlilo. I came out and told her the news. Both of us were shocked and confused. We drove back home without saying a word to each other.

We went straight to my bedroom to pray, but before we prayed, we sat in silence, looking for the words to say to God. I broke down, thinking of the cost of travelling to South Africa for treatment, and Jester said God would provide. But in my mind at that moment, I was thinking, "She does not know that my children had just been on holiday. How would they raise such a sum?" I was leaning on my own understanding, not trusting that God was greater than that sum of money. After a while, we tried again to pray. I was battling to make sense and order of the many thoughts that were going through my head.

Then I sensed the Lord remind me of the story of Lazarus, and I told Jester the words of Jesus when He heard that Lazarus was sick. He had said, *"This sickness will not end in death. No, it is for God's glory so that God's Son may be glorified through it" John 11:4 (NIV)*. In our conversation, I mentioned that I was grateful that God had kept me alive to take my children through school and that my last child had been married. I said,

"Lord if that is how you want to take me, it's all right because you have been kind to me, and I know you still love me." After saying these words, I felt a bit stronger, and we prayed together.

We sat together for a long time, and it was difficult for us both for Jester to leave, but she had to prepare to travel to the conference the next day, so she left then. Next was the need to tell my children, who were all living outside the country, this dreadful piece of news. As hard as it was, it was better to let them know without delay, so I told them in an email to a family mailing list we all belonged to. They too responded with shock but quickly moved to plan the details of my travel and treatment, including visas, because by then Zimbabweans were required to have that to travel, even South Africa.

The application required a letter from an oncologist in South Africa, confirming my appointment. Amazingly, my Lord had gone before me because my daughter and her husband, Rufaro Chitsike, a medical doctor were already living there. He was specialising in Haematology at a public hospital in Johannesburg. He discussed my case with a colleague, who wrote a letter to the Embassy for me. Within three weeks, I was able to travel to South Africa, and on the day that I arrived, I attended a scan which showed that the tumour was not on my liver but in the stomach. That was a great relief for everybody because the treatment options would have been more challenging otherwise. I praised the Lord because I thought, at the very least, this would give the doctors more time to investigate.

As I lay down to be examined, Rufaro stood outside the curtains of my bed praying for me. He said afterwards that he had seen a light shining on me and he sensed that the Lord was going to be with me. Professor Michaels, the department head, said they needed to remove the tumour and I was given a date for surgery for the following week. On the scheduled day of my surgery I had my bag packed, was ready and waiting for Rufaro to take me to hospital.

However, he called late in the afternoon to say the oncologists had decided to find out what type of tumour it was. They suspected that it was a GIST (gastro-intestinal stromal tumour) and if this was the case, then a trial drug that was effective in shrinking it could be used. Because the tumour was so large as to require removal of my entire stomach in taking it out, the drug would be a far better course of treatment.

They tried to establish this through a scope twice, but both times the results were inconclusive. After each attempt at obtaining a specimen, I had a stressful ten-day wait for the results. Conclusive confirmation that it was a GIST came after the third attempt. Although it was testing waiting for a month, while knowing that the tumour continued to grow, we were much relieved and praised God for the outcome.

God Intervenes

This news was cause for celebration because as the doctors said, in most cases, a stomach cancer that is that advanced is almost impossible to treat. I was speechless! I was reminded of this verse, *"The eternal God is your refuge, and underneath are the everlasting arms" Deuteronomy 33:27a (NIV).* Wow! It was a great day for us because that meant I could start the medication. There was still an obstacle - I was ineligible for the treatment programme according to the agreement that the South African government had with the US-based foundation supplying the drug. Only South African citizens were eligible for the trial treatment.

Again, God intervened. The oncologist appealed on my behalf on the basis that my particular GIST contributed to the research of the trial drug, and so I was admitted to the programme. The cost of this drug was R1,000 ($140) per tablet, taken daily, so to be able to receive it for free was indeed a great favour from the Lord. I had to stop and ask, "Who am I Lord that I should have such favour?"

But I remembered that the Lord had promised never to leave me nor forsake me. Johannesburg General is a training hospital, so I had been attended to by many different doctors since I had arrived. They were all wonderful men. My prayer was that the Lord would use my illness to reveal Himself to these amazing doctors who were very kind to me, yet they were from different religions. Some of those religions do not acknowledge Jesus, the Living God.

On 1 November 2007, I started taking the trial drug, Glivec, as oral chemotherapy tablets. This drug was meant to shrink the tumour so that it would be removed more easily without the complications that come with removing the whole stomach. After that, I needed to travel to South Africa every three months for review and a re-supply of my medication.

In 2010, after a scan, the oncologists decided that it had shrunk enough to be removed. Rufaro, who was also part of the team of doctors attending to me, had sent me for blood tests and a scan of my chest in preparation for surgery. The doctors found something unusual in the results and could not safely exclude the presence of a blood clot.

I had already been admitted, but the surgery was postponed due to the risk that this presented. So, I was discharged, 24 hours before the surgery was meant to have taken place. I was disappointed because, in my ignorance, I had thought that would be the end of the tumour. But then I thought that perhaps this was God's hand of protection, shielding me from something unexpected or a worse outcome. It was a reminder that He is God, and I am not, and I praised His name.

My oncologist was surprised to hear that I did not have the surgery and said, "There must be something higher." I am not sure what he had in mind, but to me, it was a recognition that God was in control of everything. Seluleko had travelled from Ireland with his son Sizwe hoping to visit me in hospital, but I was discharged, and it was even more of a blessing to be to-gether at Samu and Rufaro's. When I left the hospital, to treat the blood clotting that had delayed my surgery, I was started on a drug that required injection four times a day. As I watched Rufaro using an apple to train me how to inject myself, I could barely imagine enduring this self-inflicted pain! Life does not always give us options, does it? So, I tried, and soon I was comfortable injecting myself. Sometimes I would bleed, at other times not.

I was grateful to receive the injections from the hospital because of how costly they were. One time, I needed to buy them outside the hospital, they cost me US$300.00 for only one month. I wonder how many months I would have been able to afford them for. Again, I asked myself, "Who am I Lord that you have provided another expensive drug free of charge?" I would answer myself that I was His child, that was all I needed; to be His child through Jesus Christ. Then I would praise God with Psalm 103:2. *"Bless the Lord, O my soul, and forget not all his ben-efits" (KJV)*: God's promise.

A Big Setback

For the next six years, I went to South Africa every three months, and once a year for a scan. In October 2013, the scan showed that the tumour had shrunk enough for surgery to go ahead. An updated scan was needed to proceed, so early in January 2014, I had another done. When I went to see the doctor for the results, I was shocked to hear that the scan had shown that the cancer cells had spread to my spine and lungs.

When I left the doctor's office, I felt lost, and I wished I had someone with me, but I had gone on my own as usual. As I walked out of the hospital, it felt as if everyone's eyes were on me, looking at me with pity. It was a dark moment; made worse because I had arrived feeling the opposite - that everything was on track and the surgery would be the end of it. My mind was blank, and I did not know what to think anymore.

Whenever my son Sibs picked me up, he would typically ask how everything had gone, but that day I dreaded that question because it was hard to break the news to him. Yes, that is what happened. He asked, and I told him. He was shocked too because, after each previous visit, the report had been that the tumour had shrunk further still. Again, I was going to send an email to all my children. This time it was going to be even more difficult because it seemed as if what we had hoped for had brought us to a dead end. In my mind then I thought I had journeyed six years and the Lord had seen me through, He would do as He had planned for my life. When we arrived home, and his wife Rumbi asked how it had gone as usual, hard as it was, I had to release the news.

The next morning, I was at Sitho and Miranda's place after everyone had received the news. I told Miranda that I was going to fast and pray that day and she said she would join me. I sat in my room and thought about what I was going to ask for from the Lord. The Counsellor, the Holy Spirit, gave me the words to pray. I thought even the angels in heaven would wonder what kind of a person I was who would not be grateful for all that the Lord had done for me. All these six years that the Lord had given me living with cancer; so, I sat and listed all the things that had happened since I was diagnosed with cancer. I filled a whole page of the things that the Holy Spirit brought to mind. I was incredibly grateful, now aged 69, for having seen all the grandchildren who had been born in those six years.

Later that morning, Miranda and I met, and I shared with her what I was praying about. She played her guitar and led us in adoration, and we sang and praised the Lord. My heart was uplifted by that time of worship. After Miranda left, I continued for the rest of the day, going through the list in gratitude. Afterwards, I stood up, feeling strong, courageous and ready to face whatever answer God had for me, whether it was time to go or if He had more days for me to live.

Meanwhile, Rufaro, who had since moved to Canada with his family, remembered that a previous version of the same scan had been discussed when he was still at Johannesburg General. He suggested that I have another one done, but at the private hospital since the waiting list at the public was a month-long. It was expensive, but he and Samu decided to foot the bill for which I was very grateful. The scan was booked, and on the morning before I went for the scan, Rumbi told my grandchildren, Thandi and Nathan, that together they needed to pray for '*Gogo*' (Grandma) because she was going to have a scan done. I remember Thandi praying,

"Lord, please help Gogo so that the doctors will say every-thing is all right." It brought to mind Matthew 21:16 *"From the lips of children and infants you, Lord, have called forth your praise" (NIV).* That was a prophetic prayer because when the re-sults came out, that was precisely what the scan showed. There was no cancer cell activity, not only that, but the tumour itself was no longer visible. When I took that report to the surgeons, they decided to confirm this with a laparoscopy, an examination of my abdomen using a small camera. The obstacle was the fee. As a non-citizen I needed to pay R50,000 for the procedure, of which CIMAS, my medical aid (insurance), would only cover a small part.

When I made an inquiry, they said if I brought a letter con-firming the type of procedure, then they would decide how much to contribute. On the day of my scheduled review, I asked the surgeons for the letter. While I was trying to explain what I needed, the Consultant stopped by and said, "Wait!" He then asked one of the doctors to write a letter waiving the fees. Ap-parently, they can do that if they decide that the surgery will contribute to their research studies.

A Final Victory

That same day, having gone in for a review, I was admitted, and the procedure was done two days later. What a wonder! I had only paid a tenth of the fee. What God, apart from the Lord our God could do that? The results of the laparoscopy showed that the tumour was still there, but small and would need to be sur-gically removed. After the surgeons had checked my left adrenal gland which they had a query on, I was booked in for surgery. Part of my stomach would have to be removed, but just how much would be unknown until the surgery on the 12 June 2014. I had agreed that they should cut out as much as they saw fit and trusted in the Lord, whatever the outcome would be. The surgery started at 10:00 am, and I only came around after surgery at 4.30pm. I was anxious to hear how the surgery had gone, but I had to wait for a day while I was in ICU. On the following morning, the surgeons walked in smiling, congratulating me as they had not had to remove my whole stomach. I was very grateful to the Lord because I had not known what to expect.

Even though I had been discharged from ICU in the morning, it took the whole day to find porters to transfer me. So, I spent the afternoon without any pain relief, and I was in agony with pain by the time I was moved. On Friday evening as I entered the ward, Sibs, who had come to check on me, asked:

"Is that you Mum?"

"Yes, my son," I said.

It must have been but a whisper as I was in terrible pain. He took a photo to send to the family. The surgeons had estimated that it would take about ten days for me to be ready to leave the hospital, but, after five days, I was discharged. Everything had gone well. How could I ever say thank you enough to my Lord? I wrote a 'Thank You!' card to the surgeons and to the nursing staff before I left.

God's Provision During Cancer

When I look back at my journey through cancer, I'm amazed at how God walked with and provided for me.

1. Firstly, I could not afford to travel to South Africa and also pay my hospital bills. I praise the Lord for providing through my children who were able to meet all the financial needs. Without their encouragement and the planning that involved my welfare, travel and the treatment, life would have been tough. I have already mentioned the doctors that took care of me in South Africa. It was not a coincidence that Rufaro was working there, in that department, at that time.

2. Secondly, he provided support for me in South Africa. When I first travelled to South Africa for my treatments, I stayed with Rufaro and Samu who took care of me. At the beginning of 2010, Sibs and Rumbi also moved to South Africa. We were delighted that the two families would be together, but before long Rufaro and Samu moved to Montreal in Canada. I was amazed at the provision of God because I would have had no one to take me to the hospital. When I am in South Africa, I do not drive as I would not be able to find my way about easily. Does the word of God not tell us, *"Therefore do not to worry about tomorrow…" Matthew 6:34 (NIV)*. So, Sibs and Rumbi took over the task of taking me to the hospital from 2010 to 2013. It was a lot of work, and I praise the Lord for them.

By the Lord's plans that we do not know, Sitho and Miranda and children also moved to South Africa in 2013. There were now two families to take me to the hospital, to and from the airport and pay for my treatment. It took a lot for them to do that within their busy schedules. I was amazed at the way God ordered it. I thought of this hymn each time:

"Great is thy faithfulness, O God my Father
There is no shadow of turning with Thee
Thou changest not, Thy compassions they fail not

As Thou has been, Thou forever will be."

Lessons Learnt from my Journey with Cancer

1. *God is present even in the darkness.* Hearing that I had cancer was devastating, there is no denying it. It was so confusing because it was too sudden for me to properly process what to make of it. As the moments went by, there were a few things that came to mind, as I shared before. But it took a while to order my thoughts. Remembering the struggle that my husband went through, it became real, and thoughts flooded my mind in a jumbled sequence. It could have been worse if I had been on my own, but God provided my friend Jester to be there with me.

The lesson here is that the Lord knew about it before and He had allowed it, but His presence was there through the Holy Spirit, to kindly bring my wandering thoughts to Him even though at the time I did not realise it. I learned the importance of keeping God's word in my heart, so it could speak to me in my despair, and that as long as I allowed fear to reign, I overlooked God's promises.

2. *Prayer is paramount.* Without it I am certain that my strength would have failed. I prayed much but I still needed a lot of support from other people because I felt afraid and sometimes emotionally frail. There were people that God provided to pray for me. I had shared about my illness at Conferences and women's meetings, and prayer was offered on my behalf. I will never know everybody that prayed for me but some I knew - praying, my local congregation, my Bible study group and finally my family and my children. Knowing they were praying gave me strength and was precious as an expression of their love and care for me. Therefore, I know that the miracle of my heal-

ing is not mine alone, but it is an encouragement to the body of Christ.

3.   *God sometimes answers in ways we don't expect.* Like anyone else, I was trusting God for immediate healing, but I realised that was not God's plan for me. God has His plans for each of us and deals with us according to His will. I did see much answered prayer - His provision financially, and in providing the right people at the right time. While I delighted in answered prayer, I learned that part of the reason he allowed me to go through this journey was to know him better through suffering and to prepare me for eternity. I learnt significant truths that I would not have learnt any other way. I realised that God is merciful and loving and learnt how to see his hand in the small things that I would have overlooked.

4.   Finally, I learnt that even when there seemed to be no answer to speak sense to my troubled thoughts, it was enough to know that the Lord was good, and He was God. This scripture comes to mind. *"... to declare that the Lord is upright; he is my rock, and there is no unrighteousness in him." Psalm 92:15 (ESV)*

14

GOD'S BLESSINGS AND FAMILY REUNIONS

This book would not be complete if I did not express my gratitude to God for my family. I always say my home is international because of the diversity of the daughters and sons-in-law that God has blessed me with. The Lord has made us one. The joy, love, unity and fun that exists among us is incredible, and I can only give credit to God for this miracle. I am fully loved, respected and cared for. There is no difference between my own biological children or their spouses, I am always showered with much love. As I reflect on this, I would like to thank God for the parents of my daughters and sons-in-law, who brought them up to be who they are - sons and daughters who are indeed a gift to my family.

Travel and Adventures

We often quote from Scriptures how faithful God is in our lives. I want to share just how trustworthy He has been to me. My life echoes the author of the hymn 'Great is Thy Faithfulness'. The chorus goes;

"Great is Thy faithfulness! Great is Thy faithfulness!
Morning by morning new mercies I see;
All I have needed Thy hand hath provided—
Great is Thy faithfulness, Lord, unto me!"

As I said before, my salary at EE was not much; therefore, the extent of my travelling can only be attributed to the love and faithfulness of God. I remember after the death of my husband, one of our church members was concerned about my job and salary at EE and offered to find a teaching post for me at a school nearer to my house. I appreciated that very much, but I told him that serving the Lord regardless of the salary, fulfilled me. I felt confident that the Lord would take care of my needs because that is what He promises, *"Never will I leave you; never will I forsake you" Hebrews 13:5 (NIV).* I spoke earlier about how God met my needs beyond my imagination in blessing me with a trip to Singapore. As exciting as that was, it was only the beginning of my travels!

Trip to the Netherlands

In 2001 I travelled to the Netherlands for the Billy Graham Evangelistic Association conference, Amsterdam 2000. It was attended by and for the training of those involved in evangelism, crusades, preaching and teaching. Many ministers from Zimbabwe, including our own BICC Pastors, made up the almost ten thousand of us from mostly Third World countries. Like most of us, the Association had fully paid my travel and accommodation expenses. It was a wonderful picture of heaven - countless races, cultures and languages together praising the Lord. I experienced some of the best preachers and teachers I had ever

With Mrs Nellie Mlotshwa and our host in the Netherlands
(2000)

heard. For ten days, through seminars and workshops, we were equipped to share Christ using different methods, such as out-reach events around the Jesus Film and through tracts.

I was amazed to see the five men that had worked together with Billy Graham for fifty years. That taught me an inspiring lesson because they told us that like anyone else, they had had differences over the years, but for the sake of Jesus Christ and the gospel, they would not be divided. I know many men and women of God who have split over their differences, harming their work and witness for the gospel.

I returned to the Netherlands in 2002 for the Mennonite World Conference (MWC), which had asked BICC Zimbabwe to send three women as representatives. Mrs Nellie Mlotshwa, Barbara Nkala and I were chosen to go. We saw more of the Lord's favour because all the expenses were paid, and host families arranged for us to stay with. There were two women from Zambia and two from Malawi BICC. Five other women came from the Mennonite Churches in East Africa, including Tanzania. We were connecting to Holland from England, and we missed our flight. The following day was Queen's Day, the national day of the Netherlands, and there were many flights added to the schedule so praise the Lord we found seats on a later flight that same day.

Mrs Mlotshwa and I were hosted by the same family for the first week. The gentleman at this home was a retired Chairperson of the Horticultural Farmers Union, so he took us to the largest flower auction floors that we had ever seen. There were four floors of all types and colours of flowers. He also showed us some roses from Zimbabwe, which he said could not be grown in their country, something to do with the soil. We were thrilled to see that Zimbabwe also appears in the first world with our roses.

When we arrived there, they told us that their churches were dwindling yet churches in our countries were thriving. So, they wanted to know what they were doing wrong. We noticed that they wrote down their sermons and the minister would just read his or her notes without any explanation. There were a few things that they did differently from us, but we enjoyed worshipping together.

We travelled to many historic places, for example, to where Menno Simons lived. This is the man behind the Mennonite movement, as Martin Luther was to the Reformation in the church. We saw the first underground churches that he had started in the North of the country. After the Mennonites broke away from the Roman Catholic Church, they were persecuted, so they started businesses in the outskirts of the town of Amsterdam.

We travelled past a magnificent 32 km-long dyke, or land bridge, separating the Southern Sea from the North Sea, designed and built by one of the Mennonite men. We crossed that bridge to go to Friesland. It was interesting to note that the Friesland cows we have in Zimbabwe originate from this part of the country. The Dutch have some of the best civil engineers in the world, and we saw land reclaimed from the sea using walls, or dykes, and now used for agriculture. The main airport Schiphol was once a lake, which has now been turned into an airport runway.

Over the next two weeks, we all moved into the same accommodation, and we had a lovely time of fellowship, devotion and prayer. During the final week, we had a workshop where we studied the Bible and discussed topics that had been prepared for that time. That week was the highlight of my whole trip. We ended the last day with a communion service, which has stayed with me since that time. A long strip of paper was laid out on the floor. We all removed our shoes, stepped into a tray of paint and walked on it to symbolise our shared Christian journey as brothers and sisters.

Trip to Canada

I was turning 60 in December 2004, so my children arranged a journey for me to Canada, and to visit some of my children and grandchildren whom I had not seen for three years. On my way there, I spent some time with Seluleko and Busi in Ireland in the lovely city of Cork. It was such a blessing to be with them and see them at their home as well as meet their church friends. It was a short visit, but they were able to take me to see a few places of interest.

From there I took the short flight over the Irish Sea to the Isle of Man where Selusiwe, then still single was working in the city of Douglas. He lived near the sea, and I enjoyed that. It was good to see his church family - it is always a joy to see that children are still keeping their faith away from home. After a few days, I spent a night in Birmingham with Rumbi's parents, which was a huge blessing. Then from there, I flew to Canada to visit CJ and Dorothy, Siziwe and her two daughters Nokuthula and Langa in Hamilton, Ontario. It was a rich pleasure to be with them and the grandchildren. I enjoyed the privilege of looking after my grandchildren, spent most of my time with them, enjoying their baby stories.

One of the heartbreaking consequences of the poor political and economic situation in Zimbabwe is the physical separation of families as so many have had to leave the country. For me, this has meant missing the everyday enjoyment of my grandchildren and passing on our Zimbabwean values to them. I loved attending church with them, in particular, seeing the children attend a well-run children's ministry.

Another delight was spending a night with a retired BICC missionary, Lois Sider, at her home in Wainfleet in the Niagara region. We had met at Matopo Mission in 1961 when I was a student and she a teacher. On Saturday, she took me sightseeing, showing me an astonishing sight on the Well and Canal - locks that allow ships to move up the canal by raising and lowering the water level. Her church had invited me to preach on the following day, and afterwards, I joined her and her brother Neil's family for lunch.

We visited a lot of places of interest, but the most breath-taking was the Niagara Falls, which lies on the boundary between Canada and the United States. It is magnificent, vast, and the water flows with furious power, but not as high as the Victoria Falls. I stayed in Canada from June to December. The plan was that those who were in England would come for Christmas to celebrate my birthday, but it proved impossible to obtain travel visas at the time. That was my first time to see and touch snow, all I had ever known was frost, and I found it beautiful. I couldn't get over how brilliantly white it was.

Trip to the USA

While I was preparing to travel to Canada, my friends, the late Joe and Ann Ginder invited me to the United States, so before I left home, they helped me to obtain a travel visa. This was the same Ginder who had helped me to choose teaching instead of nursing many years previously in Mkwabeni. In October, they visited relatives in the upper Toronto area. On their way back, they picked me up in Hamilton on the way back to the US border at Buffalo. We had a joyful reunion, then drove almost nine hours to their home in Manheim in Pennsylvania. That was my first visit to the States, and I felt deeply honoured that they did this for me. I spent three weeks with them, and we visited a lot of places, including an Agricultural Show where I saw a pumpkin that weighed 60 kg! As a farm girl myself, this visit was a terrific treat.

The Ginders also took me to Messiah Village, a retirement home for BIC missionaries where I was hosted for two nights by William and Nancy Hoke. It was a privilege to meet many of the missionaries who had served in Zimbabwe, including Bishop

Arthur Climenhaga who had been known affectionately as *uN-wel'ezibomvu* on account of his ginger hair, and he had baptised me in 1956. He was a sprightly 88-year old and still remembered most of the rural churches he had visited and spoke some isiNdebele.

I was delighted to visit their church, where I observed some differences between ours and their church culture. Chief among these was how organised they were, with everyone arriving on time. We certainly need to improve on that as BICC in Zimbabwe because it is disruptive and dishonours the Lord. I had a chance to say a few words of greeting and participated in a Q&A about church life in Zimbabwe. I also attended a mid-week ladies bible study which was an eye-opener in how they supported each other in faith and life. For example, instead of being on a diet, they would donate the money that they would have spent on food to a charity.

My cousin Kwanele Ndlovu had bought me a coach ticket to visit her in Washington DC. I spent one night with her, and she took me to see the government buildings in Washington, DC. It was close to the elections, so we were not able to see all of them, but it was a wonderful experience to stand just a few hundred metres from the White House. I then flew to Birmingham, Alabama, courtesy of my cousin Nomsa and her husband, Edmond Moyo. I spent a week with them and their daughter Siboniwe at their home in the city of Moody and attended church with them on Sunday, where I relished the good preaching.

Few things give me greater pleasure when travelling than fellowship with brothers and sisters across the world. Our oneness in Christ makes it like reuniting with old friends. In Birmingham city, we visited a museum where the experience of slaves is shown in its shocking and upsetting detail.

All in all, I felt the love from both my cousins and their families in a beautiful way. I bless the Lord for that privilege.

Grandma Blessings

As parents, we always want to see where our children live so that among other things, we can pray for them with better understanding and to fill in all the gaps for online and phone conversations. I have been blessed to have had the opportunity to travel to see new grandchildren whenever they have arrived. This is not always possible so it is with unceasing gladness when I can, such as when I was able to travel to the Reading in the UK in 2010 to see Musa, Sitho and Miranda's first-born son. Just to see the face of a new baby brings such joy, and I was delighted to share this with Miranda's parents who lived nearby.

There were more blessings at the end of 2011. I travelled back to the Isle of Man to see Nomsa, born to Selusiwe and Cara. That was in December, in the middle of a wet and stormy winter, so we were indoors most of the time. Spending time with the baby was more than enough compensation, though, and my heart was full as I cradled her in my arms. I doubt if there is any grandmother or any other person for that matter who can describe the feeling very well. It is a deep and inexpressible joy. I stayed there for a month, and her parents planned to have Nomsa's dedication done before I left.

Her Pops and Nana, as they call Cara's parents, also came, so she was well-represented at her dedication. Her grandfather Roger (Pops), who is a Pastor, prayed a blessing on her. It was a lovely service. One of the nursing sisters who had attended Nomsa's birth was invited, and I understand she later gave her life to Christ. We praise God for that soul.

Miranda was due two weeks later, so I flew back to Reading. The second day after my arrival, Liz, their Pastor's wife, came and asked if I could speak at the ladies' breakfast meeting. You can imagine my shock thinking what on earth could I share with the ladies here in England? There was not much time to dwell on this, and there I was four days later, sharing and wholly dependent on God. I always marvel at the mercy of the Lord. He knew what message was relevant for that group of women who would come. I just had no clue what they needed to hear. Jesus gave me what to say, many people were touched, and we prayed for special needs at the end of our meeting.

As I was sitting at home with Musa waiting for the news of his mom, I had one of those moments where I tried to pray but worry overpowered me because she was having a caesarean section and had been gone all day. I persevered in prayer until the afternoon. A short while later, we received the excellent news that Themba had been born! It was time to kneel and praise the Lord for His goodness. This was before I adjusted to the Northern Hemisphere winters and dreaded being outside, but this was soon forgotten as Sitho came to pick us up to see the new baby at the hospital.

After six weeks, we all went to Limerick, Ireland to Seluleko and Busisiwe for their son Vuyo's dedication. I was asked to speak, on behalf of the grandparents. It felt like an enormous task, but I prayed and asked the Lord to go before me, and mercifully, He gave me words to speak. There were two dedications at the same service, the second being for the Pastor's daughter, Grace, who shared a birthday with Vuyo. It was a privilege for me to be there because it is a rare opportunity, taking into account the distance between home in Zimbabwe and where I was then. I praised the Lord, and I still do.

A few days later, the Pastor's wife Jackie asked me to speak at their ladies' meeting. That assignment is like an exam and fills me with apprehension because I never feel ready, and it every time feels like the first. I went back to the Lord because I did not know the people, so I had no way of understanding what their needs were or what challenges they faced.

My weapon is prayer, so I went back to the Lord to give me wisdom and words to say. I shared about God's provision after Ferdinand died, and the life of prayer that sustained me. When something is of the Lord, He gives sufficient grace needed for the moment, because some of the ladies responded to my words by turning to Jesus. Some ladies needed prayer afterwards, and I took down some names to continue praying for them. After all those blessings, I travelled back home to Zimbabwe.

One of the things that unites us as a family is prayer. We may be apart physically, but we always try to keep in touch through prayer. At least, twice a year, we focus a whole week praying for the needs and giving thanks for each family as they share. That means, for eight weeks, we are praying for each other in specific ways, and we have seen God respond in remarkable ways to prayer over the years. He has been tremendously gracious to us.

Family Reunions

As the different family members have followed their dreams and taken up jobs as the Lord has led them, the family has been scattered abroad. This has meant missing out on new arrivals and their growing up years, worrying over them and their children's health issues, and being limited to online and phone communication. One of our most firmly held and treasured traditions is meeting together for a family reunion every four years, since 2008.

Fish Hoek in South Africa: 2008

Our first reunion was in Fish Hoek, half an hour south of Cape Town in South Africa. When we have a reunion, we always stay in one accommodation with each family having a suite so that we can share meals and enjoy family life together for those two weeks. It is a memorable time which makes us feel as if we are home again as one big family under one roof.

There were 23 of us altogether at Fish Hoek. There were seven of my children, their spouses and my grandchildren. There is nothing to compare with the joy of that time, after many years of separation. It is indescribable. The fun, the laughter, the togetherness! It was all out of this world! There was much to fill our days, but, for me, the best part was seeing my grandchildren. Because we lived in different parts of the world, I felt deprived of seeing the various stages of their growth. The Reunion ended just before my 64th birthday, so for the first time in many years, I celebrated it over dinner with all my family. It was a double celebration to include my retirement from EE.

In Fish Hoek, we took over an entire guesthouse, which allowed the owners to go on a European holiday. It was set on a hillside, overlooking the False Bay which was 10 minutes away. Following the blessing of enjoying being together as a family, being near the sea is what I took most pleasure in. I could not swim, but I enjoyed dipping my feet into the water. That was as far as I could go!

I remembered what my late uncle uMalume Hamba told me when I was a little girl, that a dip in the sea would cure your every disease. I'm not sure about that, but having grown up in a landlocked country, this was my first time ever to wade into the sea, and I felt a joyous sense of completeness of the journey God had taken me on and of his faithfulness throughout the years. God kept us in his love and mercy in the four years after that.

A moving highlight was the visit with all my children to Robben Island, the prison island where Nelson Mandela was held for 18 of the 27 years of his imprisonment. We were all affected by the dreadful conditions of his confinement, manual

With my grandchildren at family reunion in Kalk Bay,
Western Cape (2008)

labour and the desolation of being on that inescapable island.

George in South Africa: 2012

We returned to South Africa for our 2012 reunion, meeting in George, a city on the Garden Route in the Western Cape. It was a delight not only to meet the four babies who had been added to the family since we last met, but we marvelled at how much the previous reunion babies had grown. This is the most precious aspect of the reunion to me, and the reason for it - to be under one roof as a family and sharing meals, conversations both deep and frivolous and reliving precious memories.

At our family reunions, we have what we call 'herd activities', outings that everyone participates in. One of these was to the Cango Caves in Outdshoorn, an hour and a half north of George, where I saw one of the most spectacular sights I have ever seen. The caves themselves are said to extend at least 5km underground, and I was happy to take the guide's word for it!

The sheer scale and majesty of van Zyl's Chamber inside the cave was breath-taking. The cavity is so large that choral concerts have been held within. I couldn't quite wrap my head around the fact I was inside the heart of a mountain. All I could think was, "*O LORD, how manifold are your works! In wisdom have you made them all. The earth is full of your possession*" Psalms 104:24 (NKJV).

On Sunday, we attended a nearby Pentecostal church and heard a good sermon. We received a warm welcome which gave us the sense that we were brothers and sisters in Christ. When I visit other churches, I always ask myself how visitors feel when they visit my church. The way guests are treated has a tremendous impact on them. It can affect their future relationship with that church and with God.

The absolute joy of the reunions makes the goodbye at the end that much more difficult. I try, however, to cultivate a heart full of gratitude for the opportunity, and this makes the heaviness of parting more bearable. George was no different. Two families went on to spend time with the other sides of their families, my in-laws, but the other five planned to pass through home in Bulawayo. Therefore, we organised a get-together for New Year's Day with the extended family, friends and neighbours. Traditionally, providing a whole cow for this kind of event, *ukuhlab' inkomo*, is viewed as a way of honouring your guests and so we were happy to do this.

On that day we had a short thanksgiving service because I felt that it was proper for me to acknowledge the blessing that the Lord had extended to me through my children, and for what He has done in my latter years. After that, of course, we had fellowship over a special meal that my friend and neighbour, Molly Mpofu, who runs a thriving catering business prepared for us.

For me, the event served a dual purpose; firstly, it allowed the relatives to meet the grandchildren for the first time since all my children live outside the country. Secondly, it was a way of continuing my husband's legacy of bringing extended family together for unity and fellowship. He loved people and loved hosting them in his home. So, for me, it was a way of honouring him by doing something he profoundly valued.

Orlando in Florida: 2016

The Lord continued to be gracious to us, and in August of 2016, the third family reunion was fittingly held in Reunion, Florida, USA. Not all the family members had been to the States before, so this time there was extra excitement as we prepared for the get-together. It was also going to be an opportunity for the little ones to experience Disneyland.

I travelled from Toronto, Canada on Saturday 6 August with CJ and his daughter Tania. We arrived at the airport early to make sure we would not miss our flight, especially as we would be the last to arrive at the arranged venue. I was wearing a moon boot because I had fractured my foot five weeks before the trip. It was only a two-and-a-half-hour flight, but because of the excitement, it felt longer than that. Orlando airport itself was an experience, for example after disembarking from the plane, we boarded a train that took us to the arrivals' hall. I had never seen that before!

After an exceedingly long car-hire process, we left for the rental villa, which was a thirty-five-minute drive away. The moment finally came when we arrived to a waiting crowd that greeted us with four years' worth of hugs and love. Laughter was all that could be heard from every corner, providing a joyful interruption to the younger children having supper. O, my fourteen grandchildren! How precious it was to see these Whatsapp photos come to life in the flesh before me! There were some whom I could no longer manage to lift to hug. It all felt like a dream. I had been looking forward to this for so long, but suddenly it felt too good to be true. All I could do was praise the Lord.

Some of us were exhausted after long journeys, so an early night was in order. We were in one of these big American resort homes with eleven-bedroom suites. It was just big enough to house everyone. The joy of waking up in one place and being able to see each other's faces on that first morning was indescrib-

Reading to my grandchildren at family reunion in Florida **(2016)**

Family reunion in Kalk Bay **(2008)**

Family reunion in George, South Africa (2012)
Back (l–r) (Sibhekinkosi 'Sibs', Nathan, Thandi, Rumbi, Busi, Sizwe,
Seluleko, Vuyo, Cara, Selusiwe, Nomsa
Front (l–r) Rufaro, Tawana, Ethel, Sitho, Musa, Themba, Miranda,
Siziwe, Noku, Sijabuliso 'CJ', Langa, Tania

Sons and sons-in-law 'Haka' at family reunion in Reunion,
Florida (2016)

With my daughters-in-law in Caithness, Scotland (**2017**)

With all my grandchildren at the **2016** Reunion in Florida,
(l-r) Tania, Nomsa, Langa, Noku, Ethel, Matipa, Tawana, Vuyo,
Musa, Sizwe, Simbai, Nandi, Noku, Themba, Nathan.

able. The following morning was a Sunday, and I joined those who were able to go to church. We attended Celebration Church in Kissimmee, enjoying a warm welcome and wonderful worship and preaching. It was a lovely day all round. We even welcomed a downpour which came after church as it brought relief from the searing heat.

As if that was not enough of a treat, my cousin Nomsa Moyo who lives in Alabama kindly paid us a visit together with her husband Edmund Maphendla Moyo, her son Mandla and his wife Kristen as well as their children. Their visit was such a blessing as we spent the later part of Sunday and evening with them. We deeply appreciated our time with them after so many years of not seeing each other. It was a pleasure to meet Mandla as a married man, having last seen him as a teenager. Once more, it felt as though we were all back home in Bulawayo, where we had spent many happy times together.

Of all the 'herd' activities we participated in, my highlight was the visit to the 'Experience of the Holy Land' theme park. It re-creates the architecture of and sense of being in Jerusalem in the New Testament, with the story of the birth, death and resurrection of the Lord Jesus illustrated in pictures.

We arrived just as one of several daily Communion Services was starting. It was very solemn and led by an ordained minister. Most of the workers were full-time Jewish Christian ministers. I appreciated that because it gave me a small picture of what it is like to see the Holy Land, one of the places I would most like to visit. I was richly blessed by the service. After that we watched The Passion of the Christ acted live by professional actors. We were taken on a tour of Jesus' crucifixion, and I was particularly moved by the image of the empty tomb. It was a day well spent for me.

The seven days that we spent together flew by. At each reunion we hire a local photographer to spend a few hours with us, taking a series of pictures, including some poses that have become traditional, such as the men doing a New Zealand 'Haka' war dance. These help us to preserve the memory of our time together, and with our ongoing Whatsapp family chat group allow us to extend the sense of being together.

Barcelona: 2020

As I write this, it's a warm August in St John's, Newfoundland and if all had gone according to plan I would have just returned from our 2020 reunion in Sant Andreu de Llavaneres, north of Barcelona in Spain. Unfortunately, due to the coronavirus pandemic, we have had to postpone it to next year, God-willing. The plans for each Reunion are all decided by 'the committee', formed for the occasion, which is working hard to ensure that we can meet next year. It is made up of what we jokingly call 'continental representatives' since one person from each of the continents we live in has a turn on it. They are responsible for finding a suitable venue, coordinating herd activities, meal rotas, travel plans and everything else needed to make it a success.

The committee also does the sums – how much all the food, accommodation, flights and activities will cost. The whole family then works together to share these costs as they are able to. This gives me a quiet joy because I see Ferdinand's spirit in their sacrificial sharing and the great desire to bring family together, whatever the obstacles.

A Thankful Heart

I know my words will not be enough to thank my family for their love and care for me, which goes beyond anything I could ask for. I want to take this opportunity to say the Reunions are some of the greatest gifts that my children have given me. As a parent, the joy of being with all my children and grandchildren together is immeasurable. Furthermore, with all of them living on three different continents, their children would never get to know each other, which would fill me with sadness.

I love that the Reunions are also a way to enfold all my sons- and daughters-in-law into my family. Even though most weddings took place in Bulawayo, no-one lived there afterwards, so it is precious to be able to know each other this way. Being together in-person strengthens us spiritually as we take moments to pray and worship together, share devotionals and discuss life and faith. All this would never have happened if the Lord had not poured his amazing love into their hearts. Our family's provision and protection can be found in none other than the Almighty God. My song is, *"I will give thanks to the Lord with all my heart, I will recount all of your wonderful deeds." Psalm 9:1 (ESV)*

My prayer is that my loving Lord would show me what I still need to do with the health and life that he has graciously given me. We have been given 70 years (Psalm 90:10). I am writing this at 75 and very much living in bonus years.

I think back to when as a small child I sat at my mother's feet as she read from John 1, *"In the beginning was the Word…"*. As I trace how He has gently led me throughout my life. I praise Him for not only was He there when my life began but He has been there in every devastating and triumphant moment, I know that he will be with me at the end. I stand in awe before my Maker.

15

TESTIMONIALS

I met Ethel Sibanda in 1984 at BICC Glen Norah in Harare. She was a very passionate person in teaching the Word of God during Sunday School and Bible study times. She was also committed in prayer and sound in her teaching. Fellowship with her at Glen Norah was a blessing and an inspiration to my life. Mrs Ethel Sibanda was also very passionate about evangelism and soul winning. When she moved back to Bulawayo, she served under Evangelism Explosion ministry which had a mandate to train church leaders in evangelism and soul winning. Many of our Pastors and members were trained under her hand. We give glory for the noble work she has done in the BIC Church in Zimbabwe.

Bishop Sindah Ngulube

Ethel is our eldest sister born after my two brothers. God blessed her with leadership qualities and care for as long as I can remember. She was industrious, leading us in various chores. Her care was shown when she nursed not only her husband but other members of the family. One after the other she nursed her husband, her brother-in-law and her mother-in-law in her house until their last day. We realized that her strong prayer life sustained her through difficult situations that came in her life. She is a blessing to the family and the community at large.

Elsa Masuku

Ethel Sibanda's faith stands taller than her stature. Her love for God, family, church and people in general is uncompromisingly evident for all to see. Some of us who have rubbed shoulders with her for many years appreciate her strong belief in prayer and that she seizes every opportunity to share about the love of God and what the Lord has done for her to others. Ethel is a living testimony for what it means to fear the Lord. I have always known her to be humble, diligent, loving, a servant leader and a counsellor who will give no room for sin. She definitely shines as a model for all of us to emulate.

Danisa Ndlovu

Ethel is like an older sister that I never had, my sister in Christ, my prayer partner and my teacher. I have learnt so much from her in my spiritual walk with the Lord. Her steadfastness and her perseverance in her walk with the Lord have helped me to hold on to the Word of God and never to give up. Ethel's mother was my father's sister, so we are first cousins. Whenever my aunt came to visit there was so much joy and laughter as my father and aunt rehashed the old days of their growing up together at Mazhabazha in Gwatemba, Filabusi.

My next favorite memory of Ethel is when she was a student

at Matopo Mission where we lived at the time. She and her sister Hilda came often to our house for meals and again our house was filled with joy and laughter. I was honored to be Ethel's bridesmaid when she married Ferdinand Sibanda. I remember as kids we were tickled to realise she was not going to change her last name after marriage.

We were separated for a few years when I came to the USA to go to college. I thank the Lord that He kept us safe until we reconnected again in 1981 where she played a vital role when I got married. She was the Matron of honor and her daughter Siziwe was my bridesmaid. At the time, Ethel and her family lived in Harare.

We were blessed when her husband Ferdinand's job transferred him to Bulawayo and lo and behold, they bought a house within walking distance from our house. My children and indeed my nieces have fond memories of the times and meals that were shared at their house. This time we had reconnected in our spiritual walk through weekly Bible study which helped me mature more than I can say in my spiritual walk with the Lord. I learned to read my Bible and pray with more purpose, and I grew spiritually. I also had an opportunity to observe Ethel leave secular employment and go into full time ministry winning souls for the Lord. I watched Ethel lose her husband, but she remained faithful in her walk with the Lord. We weathered a lot of storms together, but the Lord sustained us through them all.

The last thing we did together as families while in Zimbabwe was going to a Bible Camp at the end of 1999 bringing in the new decade. My son was about to leave for college in the USA. I remember Ethel's wisdom that Mandla already had the Word of God planted in him and God would watch over him while he was away from home. We went our separate ways once again when my family and I moved to the USA in 2001, but we kept in touch through prayer and through an occasional phone call. But our bond remained strong. We had an opportunity to reconnect once more almost 15 years later with all the children grown, when we met on vacation in Florida. It was once more a time of rejoicing and prayer to see how our families had grown and the blessing God has bestowed on us.

I value Ethel as my cousin, and also as my sister-in Christ. We may be living apart at this time, but we continue to pray for each other, and our families. I am truly blessed to call her my sister.

Nomsa Moyo

I would nominate Sis Ethel as the best spiritual friend, prayer partner, evangelist, counsellor, comforter and motivator to anyone in need. I was privileged to be one of her bridesmaids when she got married. Little did I know that association would result into a life-long friendship years later. What attracted me to Ethel is her love for God, and her prayerful lifestyle, that led us to become prayer partners. Ethel's greatest pillar is God and her most read book is the Bible. Her greatest business is evangelism. She never misses any opportunity to share God's Word with anyone she contacts.

Ethel's simplicity, her openness and integrity make her a friend of everyone. Her love for God's family and her own family at large is demonstrated by the way she shares the good news and gives counsel to various ones using her life experiences as a wife, mother, widow and her health journey. Ethel does not hesitate to offer her opinions, wisdom and guidance appropriately to anybody. Many have drawn desired strength from her. I am so blessed and privileged to have Ethel in my life.

Jester Mlilo

I have known Sis Ethel from the time when we fellowshipped together at Mpopoma Church in 1978. In 1979 when I got married, she sewed a beautiful two-piece costume for me as I was preparing a new wardrobe. When her family resettled in Bulawayo after their time in Harare and we were again fellowshipping together at Bulawayo Central, she encouraged a number of us and we finally started a Bible Study group under her leadership. We met every Wednesday and rotated the hosting in each other's homes. The families involved were hers, Mrs Catherine Mahaja, Mrs Jester Mlilo, Mrs Nomsa Moyo, Bishop and Mrs J R Shenk, Mrs Patience Ncube, Rev and Mrs Chidziva and our family. Later when Bishop and Mrs Danisa Ndlovu came into office they also joined us as did all the missionaries who served and stayed at Youngways Guesthouse.

She was always passionate about studying the Word and praying. I remember her encouraging us to keep prayer diaries. She said we should note and record the date when we start praying about something and remember to tick and record the date when prayer is answered. In those many years we learnt a lot and grew together as one another's keeper.

On 14 November 2017 we lost our dear daughter Samu in Winnipeg, Canada, on her 32nd birthday. Dealing with death in a family is difficult enough but when it is through suicide, the grief is relentless. People ask insensitive questions and make pointed comments. Jethro and I traveled to Canada to bring her remains back home to Zimbabwe. Sis Ethel's family provided the means for her to travel from St. Johns in Newfoundland Canada, to join our family in Winnipeg, where we held a memorial service for Samu. Sis Ethel spoke on our behalf at the memorial service because Jethro and I were too broken.

After the memorial service she stayed with us for several days – just giving us the support we needed. Samu's remains were given a place of rest at our rural home in Matopo on 22 December 2017. For the next two years after the death of Samu, Sis Ethel walked with us and continued to provide emotional and Spiritual support. Out of the blue, she would just send a message of encouragement or enquire how we were coping. She shared Scriptures or music. She remembered and wrote or phoned in November. She remembered that Christmas would never be the same and sent a word of encouragement. She did this not only for Jethro and me but for Samu's twin sister Sane and her brother Andile. She loved us unconditionally. She did not condemn. Often she would encourage us by saying "We can never understand or have answers. Only God knows." Sis Ethel experienced loss and pain, so she understood and knew how to be a comfort to us. We will never forget or underestimate her gift to our family. It is priceless.

Doris Dube

Ethel Sibanda is a faithful follower of Jesus who has always fought the good fight, run the race and kept the faith. I am confident that there is in store for her a crown of righteousness. I first think of her as a prayer warrior. My wife, Janet, was for many years a prayer partner with Ethel Sibanda. They would meet most weeks to pray for one another, for their children and their work in the Lord. That relationship meant a tremendous amount to Janet and we saw real answers to their prayers especially in our children's lives.

As a widow, Ethel did a great job of bringing up her children to be strong adults who love Jesus. Our children were good friends and Sitho worked with us as the Zimbabwe Family Impact Director for a number of years. When Family Impact was starting, Ethel was one of the founding trustees. She was always interested in the ministry, was a wise counsellor at Trust meetings and we could always count on her to be faithful in prayer in the background.

David Cunningham

In 1985, my husband was transferred to Harare and we fellowshipped at Northside Community church in Borrowdale. That is where I met Ethel Sibanda and her family. We had bought a house in Rayden Drive and Ethel and her family lived within walking distances on Maidenhead Road in Borrowdale. We joined a Bible Study group which met nearby every Wednesday. The Sibanda children and ours played together and some met for youth meetings at church. Ethel became a friend and prayer partner to me!

One incidence I remember vividly is on this one Saturday, when I was at home tidying my house and I began thinking about Ethel. I became restless and wondered what was happening to her. Finally, I dropped what I was doing and walked to her house. It was all well with her! She told me she was in the middle of tidying her wardrobe. We spent the next hour or more in prayer then had tea before goodbyes! Outside her door, she told me to wait for her while she ran back into the house! She came back with a beautiful blouse and told me she had bought two of the same kind, one for herself and one for me but that she had been forgetting to give it. I was grateful.

Christine Dawanyi

I know Mrs Ethel Sibanda from 1984 at Glen Norah BICC. She was an active member who contributed meaningfully in most church responsibilities and duties assigned to her faithfully. She helped me get established as a new pastor by showing support wherever possible. Ethel's devotion to church work was very encouraging even during threatening circumstances. It was not safe to do evangelism house to house because of the political situation at that time but she gave me a hand and we shared the gospel successfully. I also remember her for her generosity.

Rev Emmanuel Chidziva

I met Ethel Sibanda, a devout Christian, at BICC Glen Norah, in the early 1980s. She had a big family to look after, but that did not deter her from attending both Sunday School and Main Services and other church activities. She was my Sunday school teacher for a long time, and she loved teaching! Personally, I did not like Sunday school, but she encouraged me I ended up being a teacher too. Ethel was a very cheerful and ever smiling person. You would almost believe she never had any burden or care in life. Ethel also started a midweek prayer group for us at Waterfalls. The number of congregants increased, through Evangelism. Midweek prayers are still running in the area, and we thank her for that.

Robert Mthombeni

I have sat at the feet of many Sunday School Teachers, but none captivated me the way Sis Ethel did in Harare. She made the lesson come alive in a masterly fashion. All participants were engrossed as she taught. When we visited the Netherlands in 2002, I witnessed her strike conversation with a young Hollander on a short train ride, and I was intrigued by the way she shared the gospel effectively and without being rebuffed. I enjoyed sharing sleeping place with her during annual general conferences because she was a prayer warrior, and did we pray! I salute her!

Barbara Nkala

I got acquainted with Ethel through the Ministry of Evangelism Explosion. Sometimes I joined her for prayer at her workplace. Lunch time for Ethel was prayer time to tap into God's power. We read scripture, briefly shared and prayed. It dawned on me that Ethel had a great passion for the lost. No wonder she was so dedicated to Evangelism. Their teaching manual was comprehensive but simple. I could not join the Ministry because I was busy with Peace building. Many church leaders benefited from the programme of winning souls and some churches grew in leaps and bounds through her Ministry.

Nellie Mlotshwa

Mam' Ethel as many called her, became more than umzalwane (brethren), more than my mentor, because of her undying
love for God, and her unique prayer life. I developed a close relationship with here in the early 1990s when she was visiting
churches introducing Evangelism Explosion. I enrolled and became one of her students. It was then that I realised that praying
was her lifestyle. She would pray about anything and any time.
She taught me that prayer is not the words we say but a personal
relationship with God. I remember that in conferences she
would spend most of the days in the Prayer room to counsel and
pray for people with personal needs. Most times she went without meals as people had numerous needs. Mam' Ethel was humble but there was something contagious about relating to her.
You could not be close to her and remain the same. Her life was
the Word of God and Prayer.

Sibongile Ncube

I was introduced to Mrs Ethel Sibanda by the late Mr
Geshom Mhlophe who I worked with at Evangelism Explosion.
Ethel Sibanda is one of the trainers who equipped me in person
to person evangelism. I witnessed in her and was touched by
ubuntu (humanity), unpretentious love, and an unwavering
faith in God. She was always prepared to share her faith wherever she went. Mam Ethel (as she was affectionately known in
our circles had a heart to serve others. To me and my family, she
has been a mother, a prayer partner, a counselor and mentor, a
pillar of strength.

Benson Nyathi

In 1996 I had a privilege to coordinate an Evangelism Explosion 3 Clinic in Lupane. There were three EE3 teachers coming by bus, Agrippa Dube, Rev Brighton Nkoka and Rev Steve Manja. Gogo Ethel Sibanda was the only woman in the team of teachers. I noted in her a spirit of humility. I didn't know that I would be doing what she did one day. In 1997, I joined EE3 as a trainer and myy life would never be same again. Ethel taught me two great things; that we don't pray before we work but that prayer is the work. Secondly, she always said, "Jabu, don't hurry people towards an examination. Let them learn. If you do that, you love God and the people you are equipping. Ethel made sure we had eaten as we worked. Through Ethel's empowerment, the Lord blessed us and we founded Hope Ministry and Kabwe Children's Home in Binga. It's our culture to depend on God for everything because Ethel taught us that we don't work for God, but we depend on Him for everything. I never forget her saying, "Jabu, asithandazeni!" (Jabu, let us pray.)

Rev Dr Jabulani Mudenda

I am a Baptist pastor in Bulawayo. I have known Mrs Ethel Sibanda for over 20 years. She is a praying mother, sister, saint and indeed a faithful Christian. When she came from Harare to live in Bulawayo her husband was sick, but Mrs Sibanda was always praising God and encouraging some of us who were young in the Lord. She is an example of a Godly woman. I was youth pastor to six of her children. I partnered with her in Evangelism Explosion while at Bulawayo Baptist Church for many years. I saw her in good and bad health but never heard her complain nor speak evil of anyone. Her prayer life is personal but contagious to all those that are seeking to follow Christ as their Lord and personal Saviour. Thank you, Mama and may God bless you. What a joy to know and associate with you.

Rev Dr Ray Motsi

I met Ethel Sibanda more than 20 years ago in Bulawayo when we were training in Evangelism Explosion. It was a great blessing to team up with a committed godly woman who distinguished herself by allowing God to live His life through her. I was greatly challenged by her passion for intercessory prayer, evangelism and discipleship. She would always say, "It is good to win souls for the Lord, but not enough until new believers are made disciples of the Lord Jesus Christ." We are mandated to obey the Great Commission found in Matthew 28:19 and 2 Timothy 2:2. I thank God for Ethel's Christian life as she walked her talk and talked her walk. She is a woman of excellence, and strong in faith. May the Lord bless the fruit of her labour.

Bishop Brighton Nkokha

I believe that I am made from all the people I have encountered, and all the things I have experienced. Sis Ethel, as she is fondly known, entered my life when I was going through turmoil. Through the Bible Study and Evangelism sessions, I learnt and adopted important life management lessons. Ethel 's gentle and encouraging manner turned the impossible to possible and her kind words dug deep into the soul. God gives seed to the sower but gives the harvest to the receiver. I am richer for having met her.

Khesiwe Nyathi

I knew Ethel as a neighbour in Bulawayo, but she ended up being my sister in Christ. She lived and continues to live, stand and rest on the promises of God. She ministers through giving her love by visiting and sharing the Good news from the word of God and making sure the seed is established by doing follow ups. May God bless her always.

Mavis Ncube

Since I met Gogo 18 years ago, in 2002, I've known her to be genuinely loving toward virtually anyone she comes across, expressed especially in her willingness to share the gospel with them. This is a spill-over of her walk with God, clearly the dearest thing in her life. Her willingness to embrace new challenges is inspiring, such as learning to swim at around 70 years of age. I have been impressed by her humble heart, always willing to perform acts of service, done faithfully and without seeking recognition. She is a true blessing to those privileged to know her.

Rufaro Chitsike (son-in-law)

As the youngest daughter in law (not by age but by the fact that I'm married to the youngest in the family) I have known Mama the shortest time. Having lost my own mother at the age of 19, I appreciate greatly God blessing me with a mother-in-law who accepts me as I am, who treats me just as she would her own daughters, who shares in my joys and pain, who prays for me consistently (I just know she does) and loves me unconditionally. In fact, 'mother-in-law' is not fitting

...she's just Mom to me!

Miranda Mdlalose *(daughter-in-law)*

A funny memory of my mother goes back to when I was a teenager who was of course into all the trends and pop fashion. One day she bought me a cute mini skirt, only to realise that it was a tad too short for someone of my height, it ended up looking great in my closet.

I am blessed with a godly mom who lives a life of prayer and exemplifies Christian values. Growing up, there were many times I walked into her room and found her on her knees praying or sitting on the floor studying her Bible. She welcomed every visitor to our home with open arms, with those less fortunate than us sometimes leaving the house with something from the pantry. One time, I told her that she shouldn't shop in bulk because she obviously didn't understand the point. However, now having gone through life receiving and giving help to family, friends and strangers, I realize that it was I who didn't get the point.

I'm inspired by Mom to pray, to love unconditionally, to seek after the Lord. We speak daily by phone, via text and her visits are precious as she always touches so many lives around me. I take great comfort in being able to call her for prayer whenever something comes my way - good or bad!

Siziwe Mpofu *(daughter)*

What words could I possibly use to describe my mother who has been my ever- present encourager, spurring me on from near and a far? Perhaps I can reflect on some of the values she passed on to my siblings and me. I vividly recall her annual enforced 'clean-up' of our wardrobes much to our dismay, where any clothes not worn over the past half year were collected and donated to those in need. This not only planted seeds of generosity in us that would forever shape our desire to be big hearted, but it also fostered another truth in us that was important to my mother; that all material things will one day pass.

When I have been faced with challenges in life, as we all often are, I am usually reminded of how my mother consistently modelled work and faith; whether in her career in the clothing industry or as an entrepreneur sewing industrial clothing in our garage at home or indeed following her calling to serve in full time ministry, my mother worked hard. She did everything as unto the Lord, doing all that was in her power yet trusting God for total provision. I could keep going on and on, but I still wouldn't find the appropriate words to describe who our mother has been to us. We love you dearly Mama.

Sitho Mdlalose *(son)*

ABBREVIATIONS

BIC	Brethren in Christ
BICC	Brethren in Christ Church
CBC	Christian Brothers College
EEM	Evangelism Explosion Ministry
ESV	English Standard Version
GIST	Gastro-Intestinal Stromal Tumour
GMB	Grain Marketing Board
GP	General Practitioner
ICU	Intensive Care Unit
KJV	King James Version
MWC	Mennonite World Conference
NKJV	New King James Version
NIV	New International Version
NLT	New Living Translation
NUST	National University of Science and Technology
RBC	Rhodesia Broadcasting Corporation
RJC	Rhodesia Junior Certificate
TCZ	Theological College of Zimbabwe
TV	Television
UK	United Kingdom
UNISA	University of South Africa
USA	United States of America
UZ	University of Zimbabwe
ZBC	Zimbabwe Broadcasting Corporation

GLOSSARY

Abalimisi – field administrators

Akungenwa lemithwalo – no baggage when heaven bound

Amabhanga - kinks in the furrows that result from failure to correctly control or handle an ox-drawn plough

Amasi - fermented milk or curds

Emaguswini - hardwood forests making up much of Matabeleland North Province

Gogo – grandmother

Gukurahundi - a series of massacres of Ndebele civilians carried out by the Zimbabwe National Army from early 1983 to late 1987. The term in Shona language means the early rains which wash away the chaff before the spring rains.

IBhayibhili lithini? Ulibala njani? - What does the Bible say? How do you read it?

Iguni - a very popular African game mainly played by girls using stones

Indlubu - round-nuts

Inyanga - traditional healer

Imibuzo LeMpendulo - Questions and Answers

Imizi - water reeds used in Zimbabwe mostly for knitting reed mats

Iqamuk' iqolo - has a broken back

Iqhiye - head wrap

Isikusha - a dry land plant used in knitting reed mats and thatching grass

Jabu, asithandazeni! - Jabu, let us pray!

Lobola – dowry/an African custom whereby the bridegroom's family makes a payment in cattle or monetary value to the bride's family shortly before marriage.

Mnali – a missionary

Mzalwane usithathaphi isibind' esingaka - Brethren, where do you get such courage?

Ngezandla zombili - with both hands/a warm and loving welcome

Othandweni LukaJesu, Sengihlala Njalo' - In Jesus' Love, I Abide

Seka..... - 'Father of....'. A respectful way to refer to a father

Ukulaya - counselling

Ulude - a plant eaten as a vegetable

UNwel'ezibomvu - a red haired White person

Umnyankomo - a kind of a grass known for its strength. It is used for many purposes of which one is for knitting reed mats

Umphathi – a leader

Umthimba - the bridal team

Umviyo, umlugulu, isigangatsha, amaganu, umqokolo, umhlali, umkhemeswane – African wild fruits

Umzalwane - brethren

Woza Friday - Come Friday, said in expectation of a thrilling event on a Friday

Made in the USA
Middletown, DE
22 February 2021